DECONSTRUCTING THE AMERICAN MOSQUE

Akel Ismail Kahera

DECONSTRUCTING THE AMERICAN MOSQUE

Space, Gender, and Aesthetics

UNIVERSITY OF TEXAS PRESS
Austin

The publication of this book was assisted by a University Cooperative Society Subvention Grant awarded by the University of Texas at Austin.

Requests for permission to reproduce material from this work should be sent to Permissions, University of Texas Press, P.O. Box 7819, Austin, TX 78713-7819.

⊛ The paper used in this book meets the minimum requirements of ANSI/NISO Z39.48-1992 (R1997) (Permanence of Paper).

LIBRARY OF CONGRESS CATALOGING-IN-PUBLICATION DATA

Kahera, Akel Ismail, 1951–
Deconstructing the American mosque : space, gender, and aesthetics / Akel Ismail Kahera.
    p.   cm.
Includes bibliographical references and index.
ISBN 0-292-74344-0
1. Mosques—United States.   2. Architecture—United States—20th century.   I. Title.
NA5212 .K34   2002
726'.2'0973—dc21

                                       2002001045

A mes parents avec toute mon affection

Nothing is more telling of the communal fragmentation of ideas and images than the kinds of mosques people carry in their minds. It is not easy to untangle the complex network of individual and collective memories of first-generation [Muslim] immigrants. . . .

There are generally two positions held by the protagonists of a mosque as an essential presence [in North America]: one that wishes change through technology and modernity, and the other that aims for recognizable imagery. The first forms the majority and upholds change and adaptability as a strong formative force in all spheres of its newly adopted life in the non-Muslim West. And it is precisely this pursuit of novelty, as an end in itself, that has produced mosques with flying saucer domes and rocket minarets.

GULZAR HAIDER

All civilizations have experienced a decline, but in different ways; the Oriental decline is passive, the occidental decline is active. The mistake of the Orient is that it no longer thinks, the mistake of the West is that it thinks too much and erroneously. The Orient sleeps on its truths, the West lives in its errors.

FRITHJOF SCHUON

CONTENTS

LIST OF ILLUSTRATIONS

ACKNOWLEDGMENTS

This book is the outgrowth of my research and study of the formation of Muslim aesthetics in the United States over the last five decades. Each chapter introduces an incisive discourse apropos to three individual debates, which will explain the impetus behind the appearance of Muslim aesthetics in North America. The first debate concerns the opposing views held by the North American Muslim community—made up of an ethnically dissimilar body of adherents, and consisting of both immigrant and indigenous Muslims—with regard to the meaning, purpose, and function of visual religious expression. The second debate deals with the interpretation of the term "spatial *sunnah,*" which finds its origin in the architecture and function of Islam's seminal mosque: the Prophet's mosque, constructed in the seventh century C.E. at Madinah, Arabia. This debate also examines the spatial and visual affinities between American mosques and the diverse architectural and aesthetic themes that have evolved outside of Arabia since the seventh century C.E. The third debate investigates the relevance of culture, place, and identity vis-à-vis the making of contemporary religious expression in North America.

In general, these three debates inform the process and the evolution of Muslim aesthetics in the United States; in particular, they point to the roles of the architect and the individual patron or client. Each debate is complex and problematic; thus, it affects our understanding and may even disorient our sense of space and time with regard to the visual treatment of art and architecture. I hope to deconstruct these complexities in this book and, in so doing, to demonstrate different ways to understand the nuances of each debate.

In Saudi Arabia in the late seventies, I was first introduced to the rather acute problem of designing a contemporary mosque. This initial assignment occurred during my tenure as a senior architect, designer, and project manager with the international architectural firm Zuhair Fayez and Associates, based in Jeddah. At that time, Saudi Arabia was an exciting and stimulating place for a young architect like myself. Living and working in Jeddah, I was able to visit the holy cities of Makkah (Mecca) and Madinah and several medieval cities, such as Cairo, Damascus, and Fes (Fez). I also had firsthand contact with some of the finest specimens of contemporary Muslim architecture. In particular, I gained firsthand knowledge of the architectural styles of Abdel Wahed el-Wakil, Hassan Fathy, Skidmore Owings and Merrill (SOM), Perkins and Will, and a number of other well-known Arab, European, and American architects.

Over the course of two decades of professional architectural practice in the Middle East, I completed several difficult design and construction projects. My experience as project manager for the design of the Dhahran mosque for ARAMCO, and for several other mosques, and later my experience working on a major project in Cairo, forced me to consider the hypothetical design concepts of Muslim art, architecture, and urbanism.

Pursuing this interest, I took a hiatus from my professional practice to investigate these concepts in greater detail. My graduate studies at the Massachusetts Institute of Technology, and my affiliation with the Aga Khan Program for Islamic Architecture at MIT and Harvard University, allowed me to research the mosque as a building type. I also studied the philosophy of design, theories for contemporary Muslim societies, and the urbanism of medieval Muslim cities. The latter was the topic of my doctoral dissertation at Princeton University.

My research on the hermeneutics of Muslim art, architecture, and urbanism has led to several publications and the development of a handful of courses and seminars, which I now teach at the University of Texas at Austin. I would be remiss if I did not acknowledge my students, who deserve credit for many of the stimulating insights that are incorporated in this book.

The University of Texas at Austin has also provided me with several research grants to pursue advanced research related to the degree program in Islamic studies, and to lecture at scholarly symposiums at other U.S. and international institutions.

Several people have influenced my intellectual development over the years prior to the undertaking of this project. I am thankful for the opportunity I had to work with Professor Oleg Grabar (now at the Institute for

Advanced Studies, Princeton, New Jersey) during my graduate studies at MIT and later during the preparation of my doctoral dissertation at Princeton. His discussions and writing with regard to the history and theory of Muslim art, architecture, and urbanism have enabled me to put the present study into a clear perspective.

I owe a monumental debt to my mentor, Professor John Ralph Willis, who in the course of my doctoral studies at Princeton provided me with the best possible atmosphere for intellectual growth—and who showed me the way. I believe that his guidance and training have driven me to thrash out matters of profound intellectual substance in any inquiry I have undertaken.

I deeply appreciate the many stimulating talks I have had, and continue to have, with four prominent American Muslim scholars: Latif Abdulmalik, Professor of Architecture at Fashion Institute of Design; Zain Abdullah, Professor of Anthropology at Rutgers University; Sherman Abdul-Hakeem Jackson, Professor of Medieval Arabic and Islamic Law at the University of Michigan; and Aminah Beverly McCloud, Professor of Islamic Studies at DePaul University. These colleagues, among others, have contributed engaging intellectual viewpoints to my work in view of their keen understandings of the debate. Also, Muhammad Abdus-Salam of the Boston Redevelopment Authority, senior community liaison, planner, and advocate of good urban planning and design, provided me with indispensable information for the study of the Islamic Institute of Boston.

Likewise, I owe appreciation to Jim Burr, Humanities Editor at the University of Texas Press. It was a pleasure to work with Jim because of his keen management skills and his ability to bring forth excellence.

The success of this undertaking would not have been possible without the support of my beloved wife, Sulafa. Throughout the many difficult moments I faced during this project, she remained patient but always close at hand with her faithful advice and generous understanding. And finally, my precious daughters, Azizah, Zainab, Habibah, Hazar, Lina, and Amirah—all of whom I love so dearly—have unknowingly ensured that this book was completed on time. (*Alhamdulillah!*)

AIK
Austin, Texas

Introduction

THE POLEMICS OF DECONSTRUCTION

In the United States, the design and interpretation of Muslim religious art and architecture have been influenced by both the exclusion and the inclusion of historical fact, cultural bias, and a host of subtle contradictions. Each anomaly gives rise to a new discourse, and these discourses inform the corpus of this inquiry. Moreover, the American Muslim community has also claimed the freedom to compose and ultimately to forge a set of religious expressions apropos to the North American environment. The most obvious result of the freedom to compose is the generation of a new spatial form—the American mosque. My justification for the use of this idiom is explained in depth and at length below. However, the primary aim of this book is to explain the historical, cultural, and religious derivation of the themes that embody the brief history of the American mosque.

My first point concerns the use of the word "deconstruction" in the title of this book. Although adequately explained in later discussion, what I mean by this word can be briefly summarized here. First of all, it is significantly unrelated to Derrida's philosophy of deconstruction; and second, it is not an attempt to study some transitory, postmodern, nonobjective style, an abstract or whimsical mode, or an incoherent architectural subject. My use of the term "deconstruction" concerns a concrete and serious study of Muslim religious aesthetics, which in the first instance is grounded in Muslim epistemology, and in the second is related to various ways of negotiating spatial relationships between tradition and modernity in the North American environment. Above all, I am concerned with the subjective and objective use of religious symbols by American Muslims and primarily with every individual Muslim's devotion to the wisdom of the sacred text, the Qur'an.

Before Derrida's conception of deconstruction, we find a critical exposé on the art of being and doing in the philosophical writings of Ibn 'Arabi (d. 1240), Ibn Rushd (d. 1198), al-Ghazali (d. 1111), and Ibn Khaldun (d. 1406). These scholars and many others have contemplated the meanings of space, time, and being. From among them I have selected Ibn 'Arabi, using his theory of hermeneutics and creative imagination to advance the explanation of deconstruction that I adopt in this essay. I find Ibn 'Arabi's assertion about the notion of "being" poignantly relevant to the understanding of psychological space and the process of creating Muslim aesthetics. Therefore I rely on Ibn 'Arabi's thesis to decode the creative imagination of the architect and the epistemology of space, gender, and aesthetics.[1]

The nature of this formulation of deconstruction is retained in order to develop an understanding of the American mosque in terms of its relation to the material and the immaterial world. It also allows for a unique reading of the semiotics of Muslim aesthetics in North America. The overall notion of deconstruction suggests both the origins of a core and an outer shell. In other words, the opportunity exists to study the juxtaposition of traditional notions of the form and function of a religious edifice with a modern context.

I argue below that the American mosque is a legitimate religious edifice in search of new accommodation in a modern context but not to some predetermined end. This is not to suggest that because there is no consensus on the use of the term "American mosque," we can either cling to it or let it go. One way of understanding this new building type is to understand its syncretic aesthetic language, which borrows many syntactical nuances from tradition and other forms of human expression.

Allowing for the integration of syntactical nuances, the American mosque, if viewed in terms of a hybrid design language, exhibits a parallel with linguistics, where we find the emergence of a similar syncretism in a modern form of Muslim English in America. In his study "Psychology of Dialect Differentiation: The Emergence of Muslim English in America," Dr. S. Mohammad Syeed notes several social and linguistic features that he describes as the conscious engineering of social change based on various historical developments, diaspora, and borrowings from the Arabic language.

Once again, the setting in which this development takes place allows for the generation of a new idiom, which includes syntactical nuances from history, culture, and other forms of human expression. There needs to be a theoretical account of how these correspondences operate and are to be understood. In our study of the American mosque, I will discuss what role religious, cultural, historical, ethnic, or other types of correspondences have played in the formation of Muslim religious art and architecture in North America.

In the last decade, several advances have been made across all academic disciplines—history, sociology, psychology, economics, politics, law, and gender studies—with regard to the practice of Islam in the United States. Many of the recent studies seek to explain the conditions of Islamic life that are influenced in part by religious, cultural, social, and political forces. The dimensions of these forces play a part in the evident interaction between belief and religious practice. At present, the discourse seeks to interpret the self-conscious intentions and the collective consciousness that emerge in the American Muslim community. Even without an elaboration of these issues, it is clear from a comparison of the focuses of a few studies how each author defines the disparate nature of the debate.

Kathleen M. Moore's *Al-Mughtaribun [Emigrants]: American Law and the Transformation of Muslim Life in the United States* (1995) is to my knowledge the earliest attempt to discuss the transformative impact of American law on the Muslim diaspora community. The chapter on the suburban mosque is particularly informative with regard to zoning and settlement patterns and land use. Because the mosque is at odds with the Judeo-Christian tradition, it is seen by most suburban residents as a foreign religious symbol. It is subject to angry and often violent reactions from all levels of the suburban community, including the zoning board.[2]

Aminah Beverly McCloud critiques a number of social and cultural issues, tensions, and challenges in *African American Islam* (1995).[3] This essay is important because it also examines the status of women, especially African American Muslim women, and the gender relationships they encounter, which are the source of an ongoing debate.

Jane Smith's *Islam in America* (1999) is a comprehensive survey of the issues that confront the American Muslim community. Likewise, a number of published essays by Yvonne Yazbeck Haddad, especially her seminal work (co-authored by Adair T. Lummis) *Islamic Values in the United States* (1987), take up the same theme.

Since there is virtually no literature about the history of American mosques, it is hardly surprising to find the absence of a discourse on the origins and the aesthetic development of the American mosque. Nevertheless, a handful of essays have sought to explain the intrinsic relationships among religious expression, building traditions, and diaspora.[4]

In this respect, Barbara Metcalf has observed that "from Muslims in the West, we learn much about how Islam, like any historic tradition, exists in the process of redefinition and re-appropriation in new contexts."[5] She also suggests certain tensions among culture, religious identity, ethnicity, and diaspora.

> In the situations of cultural displacement or marginality in which these [Muslim] populations find themselves, characteristic Islamic themes and processes of cultural negotiation are thrown into particularly high relief. As we look at the specifically Islamic spatial expressions of these communities—the use of space, claims on space, the architecture of built forms, and conceptualizations of space—we encounter both patterns of everyday life and themes of religious imagination, broadly construed.[6]

The value of this observation is that it allows for conceptualizations of space to be identified as part of history, religious practice, and function and to be considered in the study of the American mosque. The point of confluence of these conceptualizations involves the search for a new accommodation, that is, the integration of tradition with modernity. In this essay, I will also seek to clarify the tensions between tradition and modernity. Responding to this challenge, a larger question exists with regard to the motivations of seemingly incomprehensible aesthetic treatment, spatial gestures, and the demonstration of pride that we find in a number of cases. While I have chosen not to review each case, I will make an accurate assessment of what incites the tension. In our discussion of the polemical nature of the debate, this issue is disputed insofar as it challenges conventional architectural theory. From the cases that we examine in chapters 2 and 3, one may infer a significant number of different design responses to the American mosque.

While our concern with space is problematic, the issue of design also pertains to an outstanding legal debate among a male-controlled body of Muslim jurists. For example, the legal discourse, which finds its origins in the medieval milieu, does not vitiate the importance of studying the way American Muslim women appropriate space for worship. Research conducted with the help of students in my course "The Practice of Islam in the United States" suggests that American Muslim women are indeed speaking for themselves about the role of women, the limits of male control, and female subordination, especially with regard to the rights of worship.

Thus, I will discuss the attitudes commonly upheld by the community, in view of the growing activism about the ways in which law empowers Muslim women in America. It is for this reason that I discuss the psychology of space in direct response to the issue of space and gender. The tensions between the two are particularly evident in the older, more zealous, and more traditional established concepts of space making in the Muslim world. In North America, the enthusiasm exists on the part of the American Muslim community to construct a new spatial paradigm for worship that excludes any form of gender bias. This campaign has acquired momentum, but old habits die gradually, and we must remember that custom is often stronger than law.

In an attempt to explain the apparent contradictions between space and gender, we will illustrate ways in which Islamic law promotes a more positive attitude towards equity in religious devotion. However, none of my conclusions depends on the assumption that any argument is absolutely true or totally adequate to explain the complexities that exist between space and gender.

To return to our discussion of the idiom "the American mosque," we may ask a crucial question: Will the stylistic features of the American mosque grow increasingly isolated from those of its counterpart in the Muslim world? One may cite a number of examples that suggest that over time, a regional style gains insular importance that allows the freedom for such a style to develop.

In the situation of cultural displacement and marginality in which the first-generation Muslim diaspora community in America finds itself, there is a lack of immediate contact with the past and a loss of cultural hegemony. The second and third generations may view the circumstances of life in North America with a more realistic understanding. Furthermore, the need to integrate with the larger community made up of mostly African American Muslims may provide sufficient incentive to dissuade the immigrant community from continuing to live as emissaries of a foreign country.[7]

At the same time, no building tradition is culture free, and building traditions are as much a part of cultural heritage as dress, food, music, and language. What these initial considerations delimit is the interconnection of a series of complex aesthetic, social, cultural, and religious relationships. Although the sense of time and place is vital to the hold that these relationships may exercise on the creative imagination, it also allows for the validation or the suspension of any aspect of a building tradition.

> Tradition, like history, is something that is continually being created, recreated, and remodeled in the present, even [though] it is represented as fixed and unchanging. There is no architecture without inviolable rules of construction and interpretation that are formed in the course of history for every people by means of a more or less complex convergence and superimposition of elements . . . and associations.[8]

Tradition deploys a shared language that is in part philosophical and in part metaphorical and commonplace. Many of the arguments put forward in this introduction are attempts to link the spatial concepts of a mosque with a theory of form. I begin with tradition simply because it forms one of the bases of legal reasoning in Islamic law (*shari'ah*). Tradition is useful in understanding and evaluating how knowledge passes from one generation to another, especially by word of mouth. Allowing for the precedent of tradition, we may introduce a new term: the spatial *sunnah*. The word "*sunnah*" (practice, custom, personal mannerism, model, convention, law, habit, etc.) can be substituted for "tradition." Thus, when we speak of the mosque in terms of the Prophet's *sunnah,* we convey explicit approval of the plan of the seminal mosque that was established by the Prophet and his companions. It was this spatial tradition that determined the forms and functions of later buildings. The overall argument is that any mosque that follows the *sunnah* in the same manner involves a tacit understanding of the form and function of the seminal mosque.

The interpretation of architecture and Islamic law contains multiple purposes, which require a critical analysis to expose unquestioned assumptions and inconsistencies related to history and chronology. Deconstruction, with its emphasis on the analytical relationships between epistemology, history, law, and building tradition, seeks to understand the origins of these relationships in their contexts of time and place. A great variety of spatial variants exists in each relationship, all of which are subject to interpretation. Above all, tradition allows for the interpretation of form and function.

Each interpretation brings new questions into consideration. For example: How do both form and function come to be established in a given location? Where did the builders, craftsmen, architect, etc., acquire the knowledge? How is the interpretation of form to be rationalized? These

0.1: *Islamic Cultural Center of Washington, Washington, D.C. Muhammad Rossi, architect. Photograph © 1999 by Talha Sarac. Courtesy of Talha Sarac.*

three questions are of fundamental importance to the notion of deconstruction, but from this inquiry emerges the separate problem of trying to interpret a building tradition.

In the process of preparing the research for this book, it became evident to me that there exists, not one distinct building tradition or design concept of mosque architecture in America, but an aggregate of concepts and traditions, related to one another yet aesthetically unconstrained. This impression is illustrated by the following three examples: the Washington, D.C., mosque designed by Muhammad (Abdur Rahman) Rossi (1950); the Abiquiu, New Mexico, mosque designed by Hassan Fathy (1980); and the New York City mosque designed by SOM (1990).

All three mosques are historically connected to an extrinsic aesthetic milieu; however, they exist in the same time and space — North America. A further examination of each case reveals a number of primary aesthetic conditions:

1. The edifice consists of several varieties of visual syncretic expressions, all adopted from corresponding models in the Orient — e.g., the Washington, D.C., mosque.

0.2: *Dar al-Islam mosque, Abiquiu, New Mexico. Hassan Fathy, architect. Photograph © 1999 by Ronald Baker. Courtesy of Ronald Baker.*

2. A single theme regulates the pattern language of the edifice; it remains faithful to traditional aesthetic values—e.g., the Abiquiu, New Mexico, mosque.
3. The value of modernity is apparent in the pattern language; it introduces an avant-garde expression to extant Islamic aesthetic visualization—e.g., the New York City mosque.

These three aesthetic conditions inform us about the aspirations and the predispositions of an ethnically diverse Muslim community in America. They also tell us about the intent of one person: the architect. Although the architect is accountable to the client, each edifice embodies complex aesthetic qualities and design properties that suggest aesthetic preferences; these preferences can be understood as a search for synthesis. A separate line of reasoning explains the search for synthesis; it is the transfer of ideas from one cultural context to another and from one time period to another. Both conditions imply a relationship between tradition and modernity, but the relationship may be artificial or germane.

Take for example the synthesis between tradition and modernity that is perceived in the New York mosque. By introducing an avant-garde Islamic expression, the composition of the New York mosque addresses two concurrent aesthetic problems: architectural innovation and aesthetic tenacity. The building's spatial composition interprets traditional Muslim aesthetic values, and in so doing, it sets the stage for a fresh debate concerning a new aesthetic idiom.

If we consider the critique of regionalism and its effects on architectural composition, it seems clear that the spirit of a place is a formative criterion that affects the appearance of the American mosque. Identifying the pecu-

0.3: *Islamic Cultural Center of New York, Manhattan, New York. Skidmore Owings and Merrill, architect. Photograph © 1999 by Birol Furat. Courtesy of Birol Furat.*

liarities of a place where a mosque is to be built is easy, but what is known about the spatial conditions of the edifice is nonspecific.

Thus the ensuing design process for a new mosque involves the ordering of information; however, the process may allow for the omission of what is apropos and the exclusion of information that should not be lost from memory, in exchange for the inclusion of what is artificial. For instance, it is possible to argue that the seventh-century Prophet's mosque is an archetypal building—a spatial *sunnah*—and that it therefore conveys information that has affected, and continues to affect, the planning of later buildings.[9] Because of the authority of the spatial *sunnah,* mosques built in America also embody an accepted religious practice that was established at Madinah. But taking into account that the spatial conditions of the first mosque built at Madinah no longer exist, it is best to regard the American mosque as a direct interpretation of the *sunnah* in consideration of the efficacy of time and space.

In simple terms, the American mosque is a more recent counterpart of the seminal structure, and this makes an analogy particularly pertinent between it and the theory of a spatial *sunnah,* mentioned above.[10] A few more remarks about the term "spatial *sunnah*" are necessary. The designation "spatial *sunnah*" gives clarity to the distinction and the connection between the archetypal model and the American interpretation. In other words, we may argue that the American interpretation is clearly a heuristic adaptation for two reasons: design decisions influence the objective use of space; and each design decision creates conditions for a further aesthetic interpretation.

In legal reasoning, the term "*sunnah*" is also a religious obligation; therefore, the spatial ordering of a contemporary mosque can also be shown to resemble the architecture of the archetypal model, as will be demonstrated in later discussion. Another aspect of the *sunnah* is an overall agreement or consensus (*ijma*); it must not be overlooked. Explicit examples from the *hadith* (traditional accounts of actions attributed to the Prophet Muhammad) record the behavioral mannerisms of the faithful in the assembly of a mosque; therefore, the term "spatial *sunnah*" may be substituted for the term "sanctioned enclosure" without doing detriment to the essence or meaning of the *sunnah.*

Our use of the term "spatial *sunnah*" is a theoretical formula that explores two primary design features: it examines problems of visual propriety apropos to efficacy and expression; and it examines problems of appearance and spatial obligation. For example, it is an important obligation for a community of adherents to set aside a space for communal gathering. In this book, we will discuss the aforementioned features by advocating a fresh debate pertaining to the term "spatial *sunnah.*" We will also examine a number of design complexities in consideration of the definitions of deconstruction noted above.

Unquestionably, we are drawn into an inquiry concerning design features: Are these features sensible or valid? On what account do they indicate a search for identity? Furthermore, the question of identity raises three crucial concerns: What motivates a community to adopt various aesthetic nuances? How are these nuances explained? How do they affect the outcome of a design? Attempts to redress design issues involve clients who test their conviction about aesthetic preferences by manipulating the design proposals of the architect. Design preferences are therefore subject to a wide range of opinions and outright disagreements, such as the manipulation of space, the biasing effect of gender, or the ill-defined use of visual elements.

If the aforementioned observations are correct, then the idiom "American mosque" sanctions an architectural discourse that must demonstrate nuances of architectural space, gender equity, and religious aesthetics. Therefore, I will investigate the origins of each individual nuance in order to explain aesthetic conditions that remain anomalies. This investigation leads to a crucial aspect of the debate: the belief that a theoretical stratagem found in Ibn 'Arabi's thesis can be effective when studying the metaphorical aspects of an aesthetic idiom.

2. IBN 'ARABI'S THEORY OF DECONSTRUCTION

As mentioned earlier, I have found a respectable argument for a theoretical stratagem in the philosophical writings of Ibn 'Arabi (d. 1240 c.e.), especially in his *Makkan Revelations* (*Al-Futuhat al-Makkiyah*). It was Ibn 'Arabi who first argued that creativity and its resulting object demonstrate patterns of subjectivism and objectivism. The value of Ibn 'Arabi's deconstruction lies in his thinking about the phenomenological and psychological relationship between subject and object. Ibn 'Arabi argues that the created object is not necessarily an absolute innovation, since it exists in relation to preceding products of the agent. He contends that however sophisticated the form, the image, or the object may appear, each element had been presupposed in the perceptual experience of the agent. In other words, art is not created ex nihilo. It is for this reason that Ibn 'Arabi considers the architect(s) (*arbab al-Handasah*) an authorized agent of creativity, as long as he or she has the potential to conceive specific forms, images, and beautiful objects.[11]

It may be possible that the value of Ibn 'Arabi's deconstruction of form, image, and beauty is not entirely aesthetic but metaphorical—having external and internal meaning. The same reasoning applies to properties of external and internal relationships found in the American mosque. Extant studies of the origins of Muslim aesthetics in America have not widely pursued this idea, nor have they pursued the relationship between textual exegesis (*ta'wil*), or the inner concept of being (*batin*), and the formulation of architectural composition and beauty (*jamal*).

Take for example the relationships among beauty, symmetry, and form, especially the manner in which they define the spatial qualities of the mosque. Such properties provide the initial tenets of our debate; they allow for analysis of the American mosque as a neoteric composition.

Relying on Ibn 'Arabi's terms "creativity" and "object" to evaluate the architecture of the American mosque and to probe the question of created beauty is effective inasmuch as his reasoning is directly relevant to the formulation of a neoteric composition. When Ibn 'Arabi speaks of creativity and object, he allows for the possibility that beauty—aside from being one of the attributes of God (*al-Jamal*)—also expresses qualities of created existence. He demonstrates ways in which the term "*jamal*" denotes an aesthetic appreciation of the quality of gathering spaces. *Jamal* is therefore a crucial aspect of any composition and an essential theme in any visual expression. Deconstruction allows us to examine themes of beauty or the distortion of beauty and the veracity of an aesthetic expression.

From what has been said earlier about the connections between hidden and explicit meaning, it would seem that any architectural study of the American mosque would be lacking without a consideration of the relationship between text and form. In this regard, Qur'anic exegesis, or *ta'wil*, informs the legal injunction sanctioning congregational worship (Q. 62:9). It is a criterion that makes abundantly clear the validity of worship. Another verse speaks about the notion of created existence in more explicit terms: "I have only created jinn and human beings, that they may worship Me" (Q. 51:56). By their ontological nature, humans are conscious of *tauhid* (principle of monotheism), a primary paradigm within Qur'anic cosmology. The *tauhid* paradigm considers the human being an authority figure (*khalifah fi-l'ard*), blessed by the Creator, Allah, with divine grace (*barakah*) and provided with divine guidance (*wahy*). In return, the believer demonstrates his or her obeisance and sincerity to the Creator in devotion at least five times per day.

Pursuing this line of argument, the mosque is intrinsically connected to congregational devotion, and therefore, the *masjid* (place of prostration) is a universal idea that every Muslim community recognizes. Accordingly, it is an important obligation to set aside a space for communal gathering.

The explanation of a particular Muslim religious gathering place, asserting its own aesthetic expression in America, is a relatively new idea. We can think of the American mosque as a synthesis of different visual representations in which the conditions of time and space assume a syncretic expression. In other words, beauty (*jamal*) may be conceived as a synthesis of preexisting visual expressions, and because of its unlimited use, it gives value to ideas of continuity. It is for this reason that I employ the term "*jamal*" as a metaphor, while remaining fully aware of the conditions of time and space. These conditions lead to two crucial aspects of the metaphor: composition and beauty; and the production of space.

Once more, if we apply Ibn ʿArabi's reasoning, *jamal* illustrates explicit and implicit interpretations of beauty in the formulation of space. Because metaphors are sometimes unique, connotative, or imitative, in chapter 1 we will discuss in further detail the psychological background linking precedents and antecedents—such as text, geometry, iconography, and the aesthetics of monotheism—to the interpretation of beauty. By studying each of the exegeses of the term "*masjid*," I aim to elucidate ideas and disagreements about composition and beauty and the production of space.

Finally, in the West, beauty is commonly trivialized, reduced to decoration, or equated with the insipidities of bad taste. The term "*jamal*" discloses a confrontation with banality and mediocrity, and the production of space reflects an understanding of contemplation and the need for sustained attentiveness to prayer. The interpretation of the production of space forms the basis of three polemics that require explanation because they arise from the complexities of significant spiritual values.

3. THE FIRST POLEMIC

There is an obvious need for further research on the mosque that goes beyond a vague understanding or the mere collection of spatial ordering facts. Addressing this need is one of the objectives of this book. In the mid-eighties, while I was a graduate student at MIT, I began to probe the meaning and function of vernacular aesthetic expression in Muslim religious buildings away from their center of origin, that is, the Orient. While preparing my thesis on the architecture of the West African mosque, I soon discovered that relying on historical texts alone to explain cultural anomalies proved inadequate.[12] Likewise, my comparison of past and present examples did not yield an acceptable explanation of the many spatial and aesthetic complexities that I discovered in my study of the Hausa and Fulani mosques.

Having benefited from a study of the pattern language found in these West African mosques, the present essay pursues a similar inquiry into the ways in which the American mosque is resolutely a recipient of architectural metaphors. An interesting example of the mosque as an architectural metaphor is provided in Jaan Holt's essay "Architecture and the Wall Facing Mecca." Holt identifies the design elements and the spatial ordering that are determined by the placement of the *mihrab* (indicator of the axis of prayer) and the *qiblah* wall (wall facing Makkah). He argues that by adapting a spatial ordering determined by the wall facing Makkah, rather than copying some preexisting form to suit the logical structure of the mosque, designers develop an understanding of the building's aesthetic system that can provide the essential spatial vocabulary. In his design example, Holt develops an entire space broken into parts, but the wall facing Makkah and its *mihrab* remain the two primary spatial referents.

Essentially, the pattern language of the American mosque does not appear to have any particular architectural justification aside from function. By examining the design language I find in several case studies, we may identify spatial referents in order to discuss to what extent the architect's mode of expression argues for a generative model apropos to the production of space. Furthermore, there are no absolute design solutions but, instead, largely distinct cases of client and architect moving from antithesis (*iktilaf*) towards consensus (*ijma*) to permit acceptance of a proposed design solution.

Part of the problem lies in the fact that there are skeptics who consider "Islamic architecture" to be a wholly illegitimate term; they find it to be abstract, syncretic, and deviant from more familiar Eurocentric models and labels. I believe that the appeal of secularism and the propensity to readily embrace postmodern epistemologies account for this intellectual dilemma.

Another vexing dilemma that tends to weigh against the consistent use of a functional norm or spatial ideal is the understanding of space and gender. The ways in which clients and architects have dealt with this delicate problem are sometimes distasteful, requiring that rules of some kind must exist and must be formulated as unequivocally as possible. However, in the text of the Qur'an, there is no such legal or religious imperative. Women have the right to go to the mosque, and the Prophet's mosque at Madinah had free access for both sexes, but this does not itself imply that the contemporary mosque is free from gender constraints.[13] In many traditional Muslim societies, a set of rigorous, male-formulated rules restricts the use of the mosque by women. These rules may be negligible in America because laws govern use of a public space, and other planning specifications must be met. Although the architect is free to address the problem of space and gender in the development of the plan, there has been a continuing tendency to pay lip service to women's prayer spaces. Thus, the legality of the requirement to provide adequate space for women and children is pertinent to this discussion as well.

Because architecture and art are not created ex nihilo, the argument concerning space and gender is taken up in chapter 3, where I discuss the synthesis of space, place, and public gathering. The relationship between space and gender is discussed because, although it would seem that it is simply a cultural bias, it has a significant effect on the way each mosque is planned. Furthermore, the legacy of thinking about how women use public space and the rights of public gathering is very much with us here in America.

4. THE SECOND POLEMIC

Thus far I have discussed various problems related to design and the theory of Ibn 'Arabi's terms "creativity" and "object." It follows that another way of examining the mosque deals with the matching or concordance between the building as an object and its context. The situation is particularly complicated when a mosque exists in a nontraditional context. For example, a mosque in London, New York, Paris, or Rome can respond to the immediate environment, ignoring all else, or it may engender a specific thematic concept that it seeks to preserve. It may also use a hybrid design, borrowing ideas from extant structures without ignoring its own context.[14] This discussion presents us with a dichotomy between East and West that can best

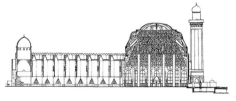
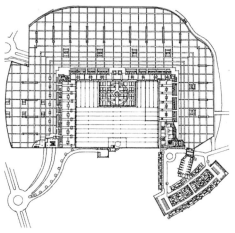

0.4 (a,b): *Proposal for the Baghdad State Mosque. Robert Venturi, architect. Drawings prepared by Qayyum Abdulmalik after Robert Venturi.*

be understood in the design responses of two prominent architects, Robert Venturi and Hassan Fathy.

Venturi's entry for the 1982 Baghdad mosque competition can be described as an aesthetic flash, instantaneously mixing one style with another. His design concept is faithful to his theory of complexity and contradiction; thus, his treatment of the mosque as a design problem is complex and contradictory.[15] Venturi's design solution for the Baghdad mosque experiments with visual ideas that enable the architect to make more effective use of his limited knowledge of Muslim aesthetic vocabularies.[16] There can be little doubt that Venturi's Baghdad solution is a heterogeneous interpretation, making the edifice hostile to a stock of traditional themes that are essentially at odds with one another. I will have more to say about this problem in chapter 2, where I discuss aesthetic complexities and transcendent forms.

A dissenting view would embrace Venturi's notion of complexity and contradiction. Although it is interesting, his spatial rationality reveals pervasive ambiguities valued merely for secular aesthetic expression rather than rational substance. It is clear that since the nineteenth century, rationalist thought has had a formative influence on objets d'art. In western intellectual tradition, it was August Schmarson who first formulated the notion of space in the 1890s. The rejection of what was natural and traditional increased with the rise of historicism. So it would seem that architects today, like Venturi, when trying to understand the space of a mosque, view the aesthetic forces that shape the mosque in an abstract sense, failing to understand that these forces are integrated under a collective belief system and normative spatial values.[17] This problem is discussed further in chapter 1, where I question how visual images travel from East to West, and precisely how various styles of Muslim art and architecture are integrated into the American landscape.

The foregoing remarks beg another question: What occurs when an architect from the East is commissioned to design a building in the West? This is exactly what occurred when Egyptian architect Hassan Fathy was asked to design a mosque and residential village at Abiquiu, New Mexico, in 1980. Fathy's mosque and educational complex (*madrasah*) represent an interesting contrast to Venturi's hybrid and egregious solution for the Baghdad mosque. Fathy's scheme appropriates ideas from the East, and it remains faithful to certain traditional building regulations that Fathy used at his Gourna project (1946) and elsewhere in the Middle East. This adaptation has its dangers as well. For example, if the traditional building process ignores

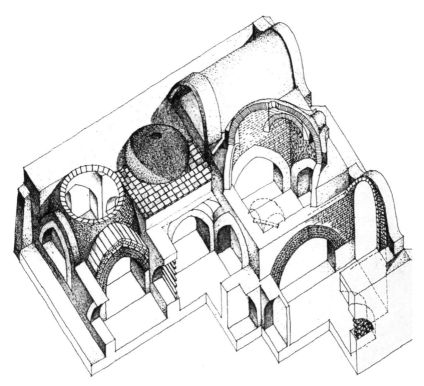

0.5: *Axonometric drawing, Dar al-Islam mosque, Abiquiu, New Mexico. Hassan Fathy, architect. Drawing prepared by Latif Abdulmalik after Hassan Fathy.*

any of the conventional practices that ensure a desired result, such as the control of an expert builder, then the building is likely to fail. To ensure that this would not occur, master masons were brought from Egypt to supervise the building technique. Fathy's master plan for the Abode of Peace (Dar al-Islam) community embodies the dominant values of an already familiar Muslim spatial ethos.

There has been much debate over the extent to which Fathy's attitude towards tectonic building traditions of ancient Nubia is generally accepted outside of its context, and over the extent to which this can be applied as a normative design value designating space and design criteria. Nevertheless, presented with the Abiquiu site as a design problem, Fathy immediately understood the underlying Muslim spatial ethos, which pertains to the concept of *Dar al-Islam*. Part of that ethos deals with memory or the neglect of memory, so that the sense of existence is created, not ignored. The New Mexico landscape provided an adequate setting for the use of Nubian building techniques and the creation of an extraordinary sense of place (genius loci). Fathy, an experienced architect, had already developed and mastered techniques of Nubian tectonic culture, which he employed at Dar al-Islam. The project illustrates alternate possibilities of existence for an American Muslim community.

5. THE THIRD POLEMIC

Although it is well established that Islam was in practice in the United States in the antebellum period, there exist virtually no serious studies on the subject of Muslim aesthetics in America.[18] There are several reasons for this lack: First, the brief history of mosque architecture in America does not exceed half a century. The earliest significant building, the Islamic Cultural Center of Washington, D.C., dates to 1950. Second, art historians prefer to study traditional models taken from earlier epochs; they think of the mosque as a special kind of Muslim religious building that is premodern. Third, extant studies of earlier mosques are not carried over to the present day, or to places outside the Muslim world; they remain limited to regions of the world where significant Muslim communities have consistently resided.

Since the essence of the mosque is a gathering space, it can be defined in more finite terms. Therefore, these observations provide a reason to study the rigors of belief and visual expression. With the mosque as with all other forms of architecture, time and space can be yoked together as part of a broader study of the nuances of belief. For example, we may view the American mosque as a particular type of space set apart for public gathering and congregational worship. To the extent that this is true, each edifice is distinct with regard to a language of form and aesthetics suggesting a meaningful spatial ethos. Just as importantly, the language of form and aesthetics also informs us about the circumstances surrounding a building's origin, its religious meaning, and the way an architect, a builder, or a patron has determined the boundaries of style. Finally, the language of form and aesthetics admits a unique genre of human characteristics related to the observance of worship, geometric themes, and structural elements.

Understanding the language of form and aesthetics is complicated because studies of what constitutes an American mosque do not exist. Because interior and exterior space and surface treatment are conditions that convey both literal and metaphorical meaning, these elements are further complicated by the fact that aesthetic expression has seldom been held in high esteem, especially among some conservative Muslim theologians. Generally, they consider aesthetic expression to be an innovation (*bid'a*).

6. DECONSTRUCTING THE AMERICAN MOSQUE

Some key questions warrant further discussion: How can today's architect arrive at a novel understanding or definition of the American mosque, apart from the idiosyncratic ways in which he or she has been trained to see and to understand? How will today's architect derive meaning from what he or she observes in the spatial paradigms of the past? This brief list of design questions is by no means finite; we will explore others in due course. However, the problem remains of the extent to which the context, singularly, affects the final product. It is a question to which we will return later. The architect is also faced with design decisions that give primacy to identity and place of origin. It is for this reason that the Orient remains a reference point that we must not ignore; it figures undeniably within our discourse. In dealing with a dichotomy between East and West, both terms represent value and truth; the building itself has a valued origin and an end condition.

When Le Corbusier made his soul-searching journey to the East in 1929, he encountered for the first time the Blue Mosque (Sultan Ahmed mosque), which he described in his book *La Voyage d'Orient*. Le Corbusier's observations would later be instrumental in the formulation of the places of worship he designed, namely, Ronchamp and La Tourette. The Ottoman mosques that dominate the skyline of Istanbul weighed heavily upon his mind, and the scale of the Blue Mosque, a majestic edifice that he included in his sketches, held sway upon Le Corbusier.

> Upon the hilltops of Stamboul [Istanbul] the shining white "Great Mosques" swell up and spread themselves out amid the spacious courtyards surrounded by neat tombs in lively cemeteries. The hans [khans] make them a tight army of little domes. . . . Stamboul was burning like a demonic offering. I heard them in their poignant mysticism before Allah, such hope! And I adored everything about them: their muteness and rigid expression, their supplication to the Unknown, and the mournful credo of their beautiful prayers. Then during the moonlit evenings and black nights of Stamboul my ear was filled by the swooning of their souls and those undulating recitals of all the muezzins on their minarets when they chant and call the devoted to prayer! Immense domes enclose the mystery of closed doors, minarets soar triumphantly sky-ward; against the whitewash of high walls dark green cypress . . . facing the mosque of Ahmed [the Blue Mosque]. . . . Inside each mosque they pray and chant. Having washed their mouths, faces, hands, and feet, they prostrate themselves before Allah, their foreheads striking the mats; with loud laments they cry out in ritual rhythms of worship. On his rostrum overlooking the expanse of the nave, crouched, upright, and facing the ground with his hands in worshipful gesture, the *imam* responds to the *imam* of the *mihrab* who leads the prayer.[19]

Le Corbusier's remarks have captured a mode of spiritual engagement, a spatial inference, and an act of worship. The following question will remain unanswered, but we may speculate: What would the outcome have been if Le Corbusier had been commissioned to design a mosque? Would it resemble Ronchamp? The manner in which daylight enters Ronchamp and the impressiveness of the space undoubtedly borrow heavily from Le Corbusier's encounter with the Blue Mosque. Le Corbusier only hints at the answers in his design of Ronchamp, which suffices to explain the value of seeing and hearing.

Architects today are often not fortunate enough to travel as Le Corbusier did. Instead, they rely on secondary sources, mainly historical texts—

which are not always analytical in content — to obtain information for a new commission. As one would imagine, the results of this shorthand approach can be devastating, mainly due to lack of basic knowledge. There are exceptions that I aim to cite, and they contribute to the discourse. However, I hasten to add that the American mosque is also stamped with a fixed quality that is both conventional and innovative. Each place of worship represents a perennial shift, paralleled with accustomed meaning and correspondence, and influenced by various creative forces, material and intellectual.

But the problem of establishing an ideal American mosque is not primarily a result of the difficulty of basic knowledge, or of weighing the relative importance of virtue, commodity, and delight (*firmitas, utilitas,* and *venustas*). It has long been argued that virtue, commodity, and delight are not enough. Rather, whether they are deliberately embracing a conventional model or taking an avant-garde design approach, laymen and architects alike are currently unable to come to terms with the relative importance of visual understanding, and this failure also affects the quality of the buildings produced. Sometimes, of course, this dilemma can have surprisingly favorable results, as one dictum suggests: "A building of high artistic merit, measured solely in visual terms, is architecture even if it's badly built."[20]

Of course, the question "What is deconstruction?" is itself a perennial, if not fundamental, philosophical subject for critical discussion. At the risk of gross oversimplification or egregious omission, one could say that the idea of deconstruction apropos to this book entails at least three aspects:

1. A careful and rigorous analysis of the points pertaining to the design of an American mosque critically addressed in this introduction.
2. An interpretation of the semantics of the term "*masjid*" — literally, a place of prostration.
3. A critique of space, gender, and aesthetics, especially how the client, patron, or architect articulates each for various reasons of paramount importance.

In the chapters that follow, these three aspects of deconstruction are studied and discussed. They inform the various ways in which the critical nature and role of the American mosque constitute an important development in the history of American architecture and in the development of Muslim aesthetics outside the traditional Muslim world.[21]

The confluence of the three crucial ideas noted above provides the structure of this essay and determines the order in which their connections are discussed. Chapter 1 plots the relationship between architecture and monotheism in terms of a shared dogma. It examines aesthetic origins and end conditions, moving back and forth between primordial spatial traditions on the one hand, and hermeneutics of the built environment on the other. As a way of proceeding from the spatial tradition established by the Prophet's *sunnah* and the Qur'an, I interpret both sources in order to uncover a tacit architectural precedent. This discourse moves the essay from an analysis of literal and symbolic meaning to the later development of a spatial *sunnah* and the introduction of a number of themes related to simulacra. In other words, it does not treat the concept of origins and end conditions as a historical idea, frozen in time. I will attempt to explain it as an evolving theme: conception, interpretation, convention, idiom, and finally, an expression of the particularities of the spatial *sunnah*.

This seems to be a valid approach to developing a discussion using specific case studies, which cannot be understood except in relation to a deconstructive interpretation of design. Chapter 2 provides a reading of image, text, and form in relation to four concrete examples, which are imbued with the search for aesthetic autonomy. This discussion allows us to accumulate a better understanding of how an edifice, while claiming tradition, is able to confront modernity as well. The case studies discussed in Chapter 2 treat various types of visual representations in terms of syncretism, geometry, and the importance of space and time.

Chapter 3 takes up the question of space, place, and public gathering as practiced in the urban mosque. Because I consider the mosque to be an urban religious institution following the thesis of Ibn Khaldun, the possibilities for social and economic intervention seem obvious. Chapter 3 addresses this aspect of urbanism. In urban public spaces, Muslim women find an increasingly broadened opportunity to assert themselves in religious practice, as they did in the seminal mosque at Madinah. A discussion of space and gender takes up this debate by disclosing the nuances of gender bias, which still operates today. In this chapter, we study two not yet constructed projects—one for Boston and one for Miami—with special emphasis on how the architect, the client, and the local site context shape them and on the extent to which the buildings provide a civic realm for the larger urban community.

The intention of this book is to examine the genesis of Muslim religious aesthetics in North America, which may well stem from the confluence of two primary modes of aesthetic reasoning: one universal and the other particular. The aesthetic image of the universal embraces conventions and places of origin; it also expresses its own mimetic essence by asserting meaning and truth. It is self-evident in its relationship to the world, and therefore, it maintains the right to exist. The particular mode of expression seeks to find its own American identity in the face of obvious social and cultural realities; it is an innovative gesture that represents novelty, change, and continuity.

When we take into account the specific nature of the Muslim community in the United States, the American mosque is a candid example of the architectural possibilities that this new religious community has introduced on the American landscape. While the American mosque admits affirmative elements of ethnicity, religion, and cultural identity, the essence and appearance of every edifice also have a valued origin. That origin—Africa, Asia, or the Middle East—is characteristic of a particular place and time. Each example, therefore, is an imagined representation with references to someone's history, but in its evolution and presence in America, it must also confront its immediate context. In so doing, each mosque establishes its own vernacular reference through spatial repetition, cultural representation, and visual affinity.

AESTHETIC
Chapter One ORIGINS AND
END CONDITIONS

1. CONCEPTION:
Aesthetics and Monotheism

In the performance of daily Muslim devotions, the repeated act of communal prostration intrinsically defines an interval of time and, invariably, a sense of space and place. Communal worship is a devotional act, and space and place can be expressed in terms of a referential cognition, which regulates the spatial order of a mosque (*masjid*).[1] While these remarks provide general information about the function of a mosque, they do not adequately explain the purpose or the meaning of spatial order. Because spatial order is both a system of aesthetics and the making of architectural space and form, an analytical discourse is required to explain the system and the modalities of architectural expression.

In a concise essay entitled "Symbols and Signs in Islamic Architecture," Oleg Grabar raises a crucial question related to the system and the modalities of architectural expression behind the development of Muslim architecture since the eighth century C.E. He asks: "What are the sources of the system, the revealed and theologically or pietistically developed statement of faith, or the evolution of visual forms over fourteen hundred years?"[2] Grabar's question prompts a fresh inquiry concerning the study of Muslim art and architecture, but there is a "danger that unique cultural experiences can much too easily be transformed into meaningless and obvious generalities."[3] From the standpoint of hermeneutics, the American mosque is a unique cultural experience. In our attempt to explain its origin and evolution, it is important that we avoid "meaningless and obvious generalities." But how do we explain what makes each building a unique expression, or what cultural or environmental conditions have led to the genesis of a particular American style? In view of the Qur'anic mention of the term "*masjid*," which also appears in the *hadith* literature, there are several ways to address this question and the issues raised by Grabar in order to decipher the meaning of spatial order. Since hermeneutics concerns itself with the analysis of structure, language, and the psychology of human response and behavior, all of these aspects are considered in our analysis of the American mosque. The aim of this chapter is to interpret the unique cultural and religious experiences that affect the modalities of architectural expression.[4] Robert Mugerauer has argued that hermeneutics offers many types of interpretation, which may provide our inquiry with a valid discourse about spatial order.

> Hermeneutics aims not so much to develop a new procedure as to clarify how understanding takes place. It appears radical and has shaken traditional approaches mainly because it attempts to show the limitations and even groundlessness of what has been taken for granted . . . because it focuses on what usually is taken as peripheral and critically brings to the foreground what usually is hidden or transformed in temporal divergences.[5]

In the introduction to this essay, I explained Ibn 'Arabi's theory of deconstruction, which may be used to explain various types of aesthetic treatment. For example, importance is attached to elements that may contain hidden meaning or those that may transform symbolic meaning, two types of modalities that can make an edifice appear anomalous to the naked eye. One good example of hidden or transformed meaning is the adaptation of two minarets in American religious edifices—in the Islamic Center of Cleveland and the Islamic Center of Greater Toledo, both in Ohio. This mode of symbolic expression is related to fifteenth- and sixteenth-century Ottoman architecture; in America, it is an aesthetic anomaly. In chapter 2, we investigate how Ibn 'Arabi's theory of subject and object is useful to our analysis of modes of expression and our attempts to explain aesthetic anomalies.[6]

Our first analysis of the American mosque is connected to the spatial order of the Prophet's mosque, built at Madinah in the year 622 C.E. At the outset, I propose three interpretations of spatial order, analogous to Ibn 'Arabi's theory of subject and object.

1.1: *Islamic Center of Cleveland, Cleveland, Ohio. Photograph © 1996 by Daud Abdul-Aziz. Courtesy of Daud Abdul-Aziz.*

1. The seminal mosque is a spatial paradigm; it is an archetype, which offers a distinct type of spatial order. Architectural convention and subjective meaning have evolved in response to this type of spatial order. In our discourse, this distinction assumes a new idiom: spatial *sunnah.*

2. Since art is not created ex nihilo, the formative themes of Muslim aesthetics suggest a dialogue between architectural form and religious practice. We may refer to the distinction between these two as a simulacrum—an artful arrangement of decorative vocabularies adapted from various kinds of spatial themes, without subjective regard for space or time.

3. The subjective use of imagery takes on importance in response to culture and environment, which means that culture and environment unfold as we study the vernacular expressions of imagery. The mosque lends itself to an ethos that connects indigenous imagery with culture and environment. This distinct ethos may assume the notion of a syncretic image—an image born of diverse cultural associations.

Since this list of three kinds of classifications is by no means exhaustive, further types of comparisons will be discussed. The design features that are apparent in the American mosque are embodied with one or more aspects

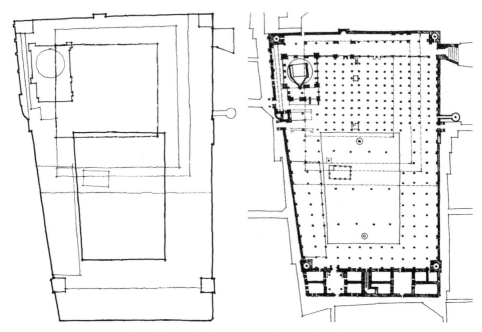

1.2 (a,b): *Composite plans of the Prophet's mosque, Madinah, Saudi Arabia. Drawings © 1998 by Latif Abdulmalik.*

of each kind of subjective or objective meaning. Because meaning is connected to an aesthetic language, which we find in extant modes of expression, the American mosque reverts to the past, even though it exists in a new environment that is different from the past. During the design process, it is possible for an architect or a client to ignore the local environment and place emphasis on the use of a subjective image in order to appease certain forms of nostalgia. This preference for image explains what is meant by the term "simulacrum." The term could also mean the religious or cultural status conferred on an edifice, or the subjective use of visual form and expression.

A simulacrum is therefore an image or an artful arrangement of images, adapted without regard for time or place. We may speak of a simulacrum in terms of three kinds of aesthetic treatment: (1) as a nostalgic reference related to memory, (2) as a historical idiom connected to a particular milieu, and (3) as a cultural or religious practice related to a building tradition. These three simulacrum themes express a dialectic relationship with regard to a building's function and image. Because the American mosque incorporates all of the above types of simulacra, it goes beyond mere function; it responds to many types of cultural references associated with memory. These types of creative expression lay emphasis on the development of visual axioms, and each axiom transforms architecture or indicates hidden meaning. The allure of modernity also contributes to nuances of subject and object. At present, a crisis exists because these nuances are at odds with each other. This crisis has led to the rise of a fresh debate, which concerns the features that are best suited to defining a contemporary mosque.[7]

In consideration of the debate, two key questions confront us: First, how do we determine what is deemed absolutely essential to the aesthetics of an American mosque? And second, is there a specific type of contemporary religious building suited to the needs of the American Muslim community? It is unlikely that an American architect or a Muslim client will arrive at a satisfactory response to both questions anytime soon. Over the past three decades, both architects and clients have been wrestling with the search for an appropriate definition. No matter what design approach is adopted, every architect must consider the importance of image. Historical knowledge is crucial to our understanding of image, and it expands our comprehension of spatial order. We will have more to say about this debate in chapters 2 and 3.

Our second evaluation of spatial order seeks to define the unique contribution that the Prophet's mosque has made to the use of technology in buildings purposely constructed or adapted for worship. The architectural outcome inherent in this development of the plan can be found in several examples, making it a compelling consideration. Succeeding religious buildings built in the first two centuries after the death of the Prophet are reminiscent of his mosque. Several of them have skillfully quoted the spatial order of the first house of worship, giving rise to the adoption (and subsequent regional adaptation) of the first architectural convention—the plan of the building. The spatial order of the plan could also be described with one phrase: spatial tradition. The phrase refers to the manner in which religious buildings are constructed, and also to an established application of skill, experience, and knowledge. The spatial tradition of the Prophet's mosque has influenced the construction of innumerable mosques, but the commonly understood plan of a mosque that exists today is a synthesis of two types of spatial traditions. The first is influenced by the fixed spatial order of the spatial *sunnah*—a hypostyle plan and enclosure having a central courtyard open to the sky. The Great Umayyad Mosque of Damascus serves as an example of this type of spatial order.

1.3: *Drawing of the Prophet's mosque, Madinah, Saudi Arabia. Drawing prepared by Latif Abdulmalik.*

The second spatial tradition is the evolution of the characteristics of the spatial *sunnah* resulting from the flexible layout of the plan. The hypostyle grid system is a columnar plan, which permits incremental adjustments to take place in many ways. Because of the ability to adjust the arrangement of the plan, a building can be altered quite easily to allow for expansion.

The Great Umayyad Mosque of Cordoba, Spain (eighth to tenth century C.E.) serves as an example of the flexibility of the system. The building has been expanded four successive times without altering the spatial order of the plan. This spatial tradition has produced a variety of examples and vernacular variations and has also allowed for the regional adaptation of the spatial *sunnah* over a short period of time. Extant examples can be found in North Africa (the mosque of Sidi 'Uqba ibn Nafi at Kairouan, seventh to thirteenth century C.E.) and in the great sub-Saharan African mosques at Jenne, Mopti, and Timbuktu (eleventh to sixteenth century C.E.).

Another type of spatial order deals with the articulation of decorative themes that were adapted from extant structures that predate Islam. The desire for aesthetic embellishment has led to commissions by wealthy and powerful patrons. This practice was developed following the encounter with other civilizations and the rapid expansion of Islam in the eighth and ninth centuries C.E. The American mosque can be described in an analogous manner; in spite of the fact that it is on the periphery of historical time and space, various types of visual themes have been adopted over the past fifty years. The one key departure is the abandonment of the hypostyle plan, which is not widely used in America because there are more sophisticated ways to support a roof without symmetrically spaced columns. Also, there is no need to arrange the space of the building in the same way designers did

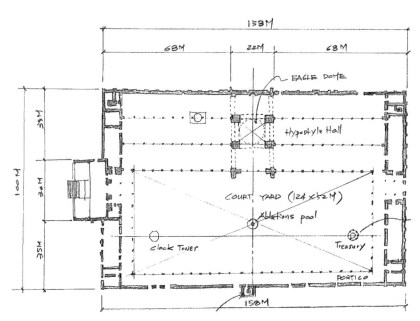

1.4: *Analysis of the Umayyad Mosque, Damascus, Syria. Drawing © 1998 by Kwan-Yong Lee.*

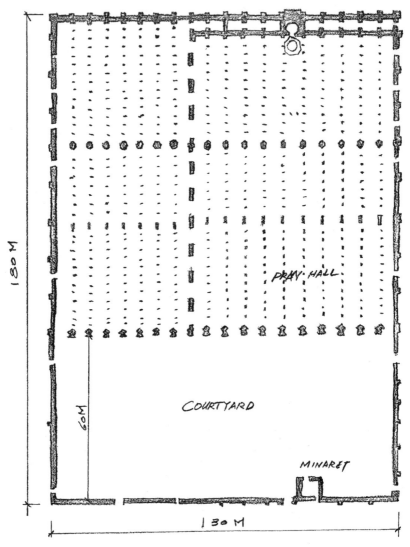

180 M

60 M

PRAY·HALL

COURTYARD

MINARET

I 30 M

1.5: *Analysis of the Umayyad Mosque, Cordoba, Spain. Drawing © 1998 by Kwan-Yong Lee.*

in the early period of Islam. The American Muslim client is typically a cadre of rich, suburban, professional immigrants who sponsor the construction of mosques and Islamic centers. Money for construction also comes from wealthy foreign patrons who continue to commission buildings with aesthetic embellishment. In this way, the client and the patron can control the image of an edifice. Many images used in these mosques draw on hybrid traditions or entirely modern themes; in both instances, cultural forces are connected to the art of building, since technique alone does not explain the origins of architectural image.

In investigating the origin of an architectural image, we find that the etymologies of key words that occur in the Qur'an and the *hadith* literature point toward what may be called the aesthetics of monotheism. Since the techniques of ornamentation and spatial order are not cultivated in one aesthetic language, and since religious dogma is often enacted through the agency of aesthetics, the term "aesthetics of monotheism" is well suited to explain the origin and end condition of an image. Undoubtedly, the widespread practice of building a mosque is related to a Qur'anic injunction to assemble for communal worship.[8] Since the Qur'an is silent in its description of the space of worship, the description is left to the *hadith*. Hence, as

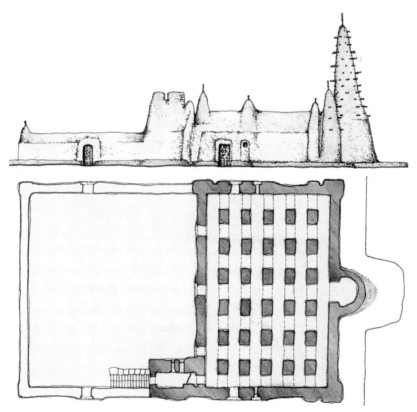

1.6: *Congregational mosque, West Africa (c. 1600). Drawing © 1994 by Latif Abdulmalik.*

we have proposed above, the spatial *sunnah* was established by the Prophet's *masjid* (mosque). In part 3 of this chapter, we undertake an in-depth discussion of the hermeneutics of the term "*masjid*."

Every community (*ummah*) is free to invoke one or more types of visual expression. This tendency is apparent in succeeding mosques because nowhere is the spatial identity of the *ummah* more apparent than in the course of designating a place for collective worship. A number of self-conscious, space-making cultural traditions have aided this practice in America. Arguably, the plan of an American edifice could be developed in a number of ways, depending on the aesthetic limitations imposed by the builder, the client, or the patron. The configuration of the site, the costs of construction, and the observation of building traditions are also factors that impose limitations on the final outcome of an edifice. In America, the design and construction of a religious edifice is clearly a heuristic process; this is obviously not a consequence of any lack of intelligence on the part of the client or architect. The design process may be the result of inherent aesthetic impulse, coupled with American building practices or other factors that defy a priori description.

In light of the foregoing remarks, it is possible to argue that the interpretations of a building tradition and the spatial features affect the design of a mosque, since they result from a diversity of origins. In accordance with this general argument, one type of form-making code finds its origin in the Qur'an and the *hadith*. Take for example the injunction that controls the *qiblah* axis. Although the *qiblah* axis is often defined as the axis of prayer or the ontological axis, it is the Qur'anic injunction that governs the orientation of an edifice and, ipso facto, requires that all devotees face the direction of Makkah.[9] Since the design of a modern religious edifice considers this injunction as well, we will discuss how the *qiblah* is accommodated in site planning in the American context.[10] Any effective discussion of the process would need to explain the relationship between the *qiblah* as a form-making code and the method of site planning. Architectural form and spatial order can be explained as a two-tiered procedure based on building codes or design objectives and form-making codes, which find their origins in the religious text.

A careful examination of textual references suggests religious or cultural meaning; for example, the idiom "aesthetics of monotheism" is affected by religious belief. However, we may question the narrow view of Western art-historicism and suggest a radical shift that takes into account religious belief and culture. Postmodernist theory has excluded this sort of consideration from its thinking, and furthermore, it views religion in a negative light. In general, postmodern thought emphasizes abstraction, which renders experience or sensory perception devoid of cultural meaning. In any case, a better model for thinking about Muslim religious aesthetics in North America reflects on the aesthetics of monotheism. This reflection is important because it is obviously part of the experience of every Muslim community and is also an expression of human identity. The American community understands that the mosque owes its valued origin to the norms of space established by the archetypal edifice, which was built by the Prophet and his companions. If we set aside the type of materials used and the techniques of construction, a mosque built today in the United States is in many ways a regional variation of the archetypal mosque. The level of analysis taken up in chapter 2 explains the decoding of aesthetic variations. The discussion here has set the course for a debate about a neoteric architectural genre, which we call the American mosque. Part 2 of this chapter explains in further detail the concepts discussed above, beginning with a discussion about the hermeneutics of the term "*masjid*."

2. INTERPRETATION:
Hermeneutics and the Meaning of the Word "Masjid"

Although I have argued above that textual meaning and architectural form can be expressed in the idiom "aesthetics of monotheism," a second consideration informs the idiom with regard to time and space. This consideration relates to the extent to which time and space are reflected in the hermeneutics of the word "*masjid*." We will now undertake an in-depth inquiry of the word in order to explore another unique connection between the production of architectural space and textual meaning. In terms of the translation from text to form, a sanctioned *hadith* offers an interpretation of time and space that captures the universal essence of a mosque: "The [whole] earth is a *masjid* for you, so wherever you are at the time of prayer, make your prostration there."[11]

Undoubtedly, the *hadith* gives primary consideration to the importance of devotion, but it also qualifies the spatial environment of a mosque and the constraints of its aesthetic treatment. Exploring the form of an edifice, the weight of the *hadith* yields aesthetic possibilities, which are expressed or understood by analogy. Our foremost analogy is an exegesis that is grounded in a Qur'anic paradigm; it sanctions the belief that the earth is a divine manifestation of Allah, the Creator and the Master Builder of all creation. In the absence of a man-made enclosure set aside for worship, the immense structural dome of the sky can be perceived as a symbolic architectural form, which encompasses a worshipper in an open field.[12] A second analogy explains the constraints of aesthetic treatment. The Qur'anic text corroborates the aesthetic treatment of space and form by making it obligatory to build or maintain an edifice solely for the purpose of worship. The following verse illustrates the injunction to erect and preserve a religious edifice: "The mosques of Allah shall be visited and maintained ['*amara*] by those who believe in Allah and the last day, and establish regular prayers . . ." (Q. 9:18).

Although the verse highlights the lexical definition of a mosque, it also brings out a number of points. First, the term "'*amara*" (to build, to maintain, to restore, to preserve, to refurbish) implies the obligation to construct and preserve the physical quality of the edifice ('*imara*). Second, the term "'*amara*" makes it known that the prime objective of an edifice is to promote regular communal devotion since it is to be visited regularly and maintained. Finally, the term "'*amara*" allows us to locate the textual meaning apropos to the primordial form of a mosque. We have defined the primordial form as a spatial *sunnah;* this definition is discussed in further detail below.

Consideration of the term "'*amara*" also points to the extreme care that a religious edifice demands. The Qur'an also addresses this importance elsewhere: "Did not Allah check one set of people with another, edifices [monasteries, churches, synagogues, and mosques] would surely have been pulled down [*hudimat*] in which the name of Allah is commemorated in abundant measure" (Q. 22:40). The term "*hadama*" (to tear down, to demolish, to destroy, to dilapidate) makes it relatively easy to envision why the first verse stresses the obligation to build and maintain; it is purposely to avoid the disintegration of communal devotion and divine remembrance.

The Qur'anic mention of the term "'*amara*" would seem to support the indispensable need to establish a prescribed type of religious enclosure. However, from the viewpoint of the Qur'an, religious devotion is not contingent upon a prescribed place of worship, and furthermore, architectural intervention fulfills a subordinate purpose.

It is for this reason that the declaration "The [whole] earth is a *masjid*" negates the need for a fixed or singularly prescriptive type of enclosure. Rather, it places emphasis solely on the act, time, and place of prostration. Therefore, we may say that any spatial form that is erected is simply the result of a secondary effort by a single architect. In terms of a prescribed space set aside for devotion, it is therefore deceptive to speak of the architect as the creator of any original form or ideal enclosure. However, in light of the obligation to build, it is possible to identify certain types of buildings modeled after the seventh-century Prophet's mosque that represent the efficacy of the textual term "*'amara*."

Another interpretation accounts for the etymology of the word "*masjid*" by making it analogous to the act, time, and space of prostration. In this interpretation, the word "*masjid*" is derived from the Arabic verb "*sa-ja-da*," meaning "to prostrate or to bow down in worship to God." While the spatial cognition of a physical space is proved by this etymology, the incident of individual or communal prostration remains far more meaningful. When undertaking a discussion of the mosque as a building type, most art historians have hardly explained the lexical definition of the term "*masjid*" as we have done here.[13] There are certainly some ontological difficulties with the definition that may have caused them to avoid any attempts to explain its textual meaning. For example, if we join the above mentioned *hadith* with one that describes the building of the Prophet's mosque, we are actually referring to two basic types of spatial enclosures: one specified and the other indeterminate. However, conventional usage has always meant a specified space. Part of the problem lies in the fact that the original archetypal building no longer exists for us to study, and very few attempts have been made to reconstruct the evolution of the building. We can only base our understanding of the original structure on a close reading of the *hadith*. The following *hadith* describes the primary spatial characteristics of the Prophet's mosque.

In the lifetime of Allah's Apostle [the Prophet Muhammad] [his] mosque was built of adobe. The roof of the leaves of date palms. Abu Bakr did not alter it, Umar expanded it on the same pattern as it was in the lifetime of the Prophet, by using adobe, leaves of date palms and changing the pillars into wooden ones. Uthman changed it by expanding it to a great extent and built its walls with engraved stones and lime and made its pillars with engraved stones and its roof of teak-wood.[14]

The text of the *hadith* admits that the architectural and structural configuration of the Prophet's mosque exhibited hardly any attention to adornment or beautification. It would appear that the architectural configuration was essentially a functional space without the use of ornament or inscription, having the single architectural purpose of meeting domestic and devotional requirements. One devotional requirement was the orientation (*qiblah*) of the building. At the time of its construction, the mosque was oriented northward toward Bait al-Maqdis (Jerusalem). Even in a most rudimentary setting, the place of prostration (*sujud*) retains an association with the ontological axis, the *qiblah,* which orients a worshipper or an edifice in the direction of the Ka'bah at Makkah.[15] *Masajid* everywhere in the world adhere to this ontological rule; it is both an esoteric affirmation and a universal expression of belief.[16] The indicator of the *qiblah,* the *mihrab,* may be expressed in two principal modes: as a simple, demarcated niche on the ground indicating the *qiblah,* or as an embellished vertical element in the *qiblah* wall of a religious edifice. But as an ontological axis, both the *qiblah* and the *mihrab* are decidedly understood by the community of believers (*ummah*).[17]

The *mihrab* symbolizes an aesthetic expression, and this symbolism endorses the adherence to a prescribed mode of devotion. Further manifestations of various indigenous expressions of the *mihrab* are also evident in myriad regional and ethnic architectural idioms.

Another *hadith* makes clear a few more devotional characteristics of the building.

> The Messenger of Allah [Prophet Muhammad] came to Madinah and stayed in the upper part of Madinah for fourteen nights with a tribe called Banu Amr ibn Auf. He then sent for the chiefs of Banu al-Najjar and they came. He then ordered a mosque to be built. Trees were [cut and thus] placed in rows towards the *qiblah* and stones were set forth on both sides of the door [and while building the mosque] they [the companions] sang with the Prophet.[18]

According to Nur al-Din al-Samhudi, the original plan of the building was a rectangular enclosure measuring approximately sixty cubits by seventy cubits, with doors pierced in the eastern and western walls.[19] It contained a colonnade or shaded portico (*zullah*) consisting of palm-trunk columns along the northern wall, where devotees could gather to worship.

1.7: *A simple **mihrab**, Taif, Saudi Arabia. Photograph © 1980 by Akel Ismail Kahera.*

Regularly spaced palm trunks supported the thatched roof of the portico. Sixteen or seventeen months after the Prophet's migration to Madinah, the axis of prayer (*qiblah*) was changed from Jerusalem to Makkah following a Qur'anic revelation that resulted in the alteration of the southern wall.[20] A shaded portico was added along this wall from east to west facing Makkah. It consisted of a colonnade of palm-trunk columns quite similar to that of the northern portico, and it served as a sanctuary for the performance of prayer. The sanctuary contained several liturgical elements, which have come to form the basis of mosque architecture and have been adopted extensively in various stylistic and regional renditions of the building. Some of these elements are rendered quite beautifully in a poem by Hassan ibn Thabit.

> In Madinah there are still traces of the Messenger, and a luminous abode
>   of gathering—though traces may disappear and perish.
> The signs of a sacred house [*dar hurma*] are not effaced; in it the Guide's
>   pulpit [*minbar*], which he used to ascend.
> Plain are the traces and lasting the landmarks; in his quarters [*rab*] a prayer
>   place and a mosque.
> And the mosque which longs for his presence became desolate with only
>   his *maqam* [station or place of standing] and *maq'ad* [place of sitting on
>   the *minbar*] remaining as memorials.
> In it are enclosures [*hujurat*] wherein would descend God's light brilliant
>   and bright.[21]

In addition, the building had adjacent residential quarters for the Prophet and his family, but these were later demolished after the death of the Prophet in 632 C.E. to make room for expansion of the mosque. In the original structure, nine adjacent rooms were used as private domestic quarters. In the time of the Prophet, the rooms were spatially contiguous with the prayer sanctuary and were entered by way of the sanctuary. It is in regard to the requirement of privacy that the Qur'anic chapter *surah al-Hujurat,* or "The Inner Apartments," was revealed to the Prophet. The verses of *surah al-Hujurat* caution the Prophet's companions about "lowering their voices in the presence of Allah's Messenger . . . and refraining from shout[ing] to the Prophet from outside of the inner apartments" (Q. 49:3–6).

Following the change of the *qiblah* direction, the northern portico, or *zullah,* became a permanent place for the poor and the weary to rest or engage in worship and the recitation of the Qur'an. Many of the Prophet's companions gave up their worldly interests and engaged themselves in a life of retirement devoted to the service of God (*zuhud*) under the shade of the portico. As mentioned above, the portico was lined with columns, which were spaced at regular intervals to support the roof structure.

The companions who frequented the portico were known as *ahl al-Suffah* or *ashab al-Suffah* (literally, people of the ledge or portico). The courtyard of the building was often used as a civic space, and on one occasion a group of Abyssinians performed a sword-and-lances dance for an audience that included the Prophet and his wife Ayesha. The building also functioned as a place for congregational worship on Fridays, the day of assembly (*yawm al-Jum'ah*), when the people came to hear the Prophet deliver the *khutbah*, or sermon. As the crowds grew, a *minbar*, or raised platform, of three steps was introduced to make it easier for the Prophet to be heard and seen. The *adhan* (call to prayer) was pronounced from the roof of the building, since there was no *manarah*, or minaret. This humble structure became the paradigm for future *masajid*, which were built following the spread of Islam in the first century after the death of the Prophet Muhammad. Later *masajid* demonstrate a regional development and refinement of the Madinah prototype. Regional building traditions outside Madinah had a direct influence on the early development of other mosques and on the aesthetic relationship between what was perceived by convention to be modeled after the Madinah prototype and what was the result of regional influence. The Madinah prototype was conveniently modified to accept idiosyncratic aesthetic themes found in later regional models.

3. CONVENTION:
The Spatial Sunnah *as Archetype*

So far, we have considered the textual meaning and traced the development of the archetypal mosque. In the next aspect of the discussion, I would like to explore the hermeneutics of the term "spatial *sunnah*," in light of the fact that the first mosque was a humble building. The word "*sunnah*" itself in Arabic has many meanings: norm; a legally binding precedent sanctioned by tradition; habitual and customary practice or procedure; exemplar; and mannerism.[22] The idiom "spatial *sunnah*" emphasizes the spatial norms sanctioned by the Prophet and his companions, hence the conventional use of the same grid plan and architectural elements that we encounter in succeeding mosques.

The fundamental purpose of defining the space of the seminal mosque by using the term "spatial *sunnah*" is not to suggest an absolute definition but rather to identify the general characteristics of the edifice apropos to the acceptance of orthodox belief, so that we can discuss its functional aspects accurately. Because the Prophet's mosque laid the foundation for the elements of the space, it can be regarded as a nascent structure. Hence it proved acceptable as a legally binding precedent in the first instance following the importance of the Prophet's *sunnah*. However, over time we find that a fundamental architecture of the grid developed that was clearly related to cultural or regional adaptation. This change was due to the subsequent proliferation of architectural features that predate the history of the seminal mosque. The notion of adaptation is discussed in the subsequent parts of this chapter, where I present a fuller description and interpretation of various modes of adaptation.

The idiom "spatial *sunnah*" is consistent with references made in al-Samhudi's narrative.[23] As an example, it reflects a wide understanding of the features of the original structure that were adapted in succeeding structures; it is thus clear that the original mosque served as an exemplary edifice. The spatial *sunnah* was so popular and widespread that after the death of the Prophet, the formative themes of subsequent religious buildings emulated the planned order of the Prophet's mosque. It progressively became the practice to adapt one or more aspects of the original building, thereby engendering the appearance of an important feature of the Prophet's *sunnah*.

The affinity of the Prophet's mosque to later buildings is crucial because it informs the tacit meaning that underlies the spatial essence of a mosque. The affinity would seem to offer a reasonable definition bound by the *hadith*, and it would seem to suggest a convincing reason to accept the term "spatial *sunnah*" as the spatial essence of the Prophet's mosque. It is possible to argue that the spatial essence of the archetypal structure takes precedence over any type of art-historical value. But such a contention is highly complex in light of the extant literature that gives emphasis to the art history of later mosques. In addition, the attribution of the idiom "spatial *sunnah*," despite its controversial aspects, is of fundamental importance to an emerging architectural theory. In the *hadith,* the prime injunctions concerning spatial conduct seem to denote a general theory of spatial mannerism. Many references can be found in the *hadith* concerning personal decorum within the

1.8: *Mihrab, Islamic Center of Central Jersey, Monmouth Junction, New Jersey. Photograph © 1999 by Asad Siddiqui. Courtesy of Asad Siddiqui.*

confines of a mosque. Without exaggerating the merits of the *hadith,* it is clear that the boundaries between behavior and the physical features of the mosque are not only clear but also certain.

We may also define the idiom "spatial *sunnah*" in terms of a design theory, making it the central mechanism of creativity or essential to the construction of a humble building. It is doubtful whether the term "spatial *sunnah*" would find unanimous agreement among contemporary architects, since any architect would still be faced with the need to support a proposed version of a mosque plan with sufficient spatial evidence of the *sunnah.*

Finally, because new physical elements were later added to the initial structure—for example, the dome, the minaret, and the *mihrab*—we are faced with a dilemma of deciding whether it is legitimate or not to record these elements as being original. Hence, the discussion of the treatment of space reveals areas that are neither straightforward nor easy to understand. It is for this reason that the designer of a contemporary mosque in America faces special problems in trying to simulate the physical details of extant regional examples while little value is placed on the fundamental elements of the spatial *sunnah.*

The affinity between the criteria of worship and the term "spatial *sunnah*" is cognate to three hypotheses: (1) that the *masjid* is a humble structure, (2) that the *masjid* is a configured space without a prescribed structure, and (3) that the *masjid* is a humble space determined for worship. These hypotheses warrant further discussion. Since it is widely agreed that mosques everywhere owe their origin to the archetypal mosque at Madinah, the most obvious aspect of the physical attributes of a building has to do with the spatial inference and function. However, in an effort to explain how later mosques have emerged, art historians have generally focused on individual patrons and stylistic details, treating the mosque as a work of art; but they have essentially ignored the primordial spatial relationship. Some art historians have even stated that the Prophet's mosque was only a house.

A greater difficulty lies in the consideration of hybrid aesthetics, which point to the existence of a range of architectural problems that are important to our study of the American mosque. As noted above, a range of possible explanations exists for studying the mosque as a regional building type. Hence, the functional aspect of the American mosque tends to confirm the hypothesis of a spatial *sunnah,* even though the architectural features have only been developed over the past five decades. This development has not

1.9: *Detail of tile work, Ranchos mosque, Abiquiu, New Mexico. Photograph © 1999 by Ronald Baker. Courtesy of Ronald Baker.*

been influenced by a single design theory but is rather the result of a complex process. For example, it is well known in the United States that most architects who have been hired to construct a mosque do not have encyclopedic mastery of the relevant planning or historical data. Establishing the concept of a spatial *sunnah* is essential because the search for a model can be confused by the features of hybrid examples whose origins often predate Islam. An excellent example is the Great Umayyad mosque of Damascus (eighth century C.E.). The aesthetics of the Damascus mosque raise issues that distort the idiom "spatial *sunnah*" because the mosque entertains the use of ornamental features, while retaining a functional affinity with the primordial edifice. Because of its eclectic nature, the Damascus mosque is a simulacrum, a hybrid image whose structural elements have been adapted from Roman and Byzantine edifices.

Along with the Damascus mosque, many novel aesthetic features emerged after the conquest of lands outside of Arabia, and the hybrid features of each configuration display an aesthetic quality that can best be described as a simulacrum, or an artful arrangement of aesthetic elements.

4. IDIOM:
Themes of Simulacra and West African Aesthetics

In the foregoing discussion, we described the form and spatial elements of the archetypal edifice as having an adaptable grid plan. It could be argued that later buildings demonstrate an evolution of the same expression in the development of mosque architecture. Through this development, specific examples of building types have evolved over time. The subsequent practice of recycling part or all of a preexisting structure serves to confirm the hypothesis that the evolution of an edifice is relative to the term "*'amara*" (to build and maintain). A retrofitted building is controlled by two important criteria: function and orientation to Makkah. The process of reconstruction and adaptive reuse has led to a variety of regional examples. For instance, the Great Mosque of Kairouan (eighth century C.E. and later, built on a site founded by Sidi 'Uqba ibn Nafi) is an edifice that has been developed through the use of Roman and Byzantine structural elements integrated into a hypostyle plan. The combination of ornament is a composite treatment of styles. Paul Sebag describes the eclectic treatment:

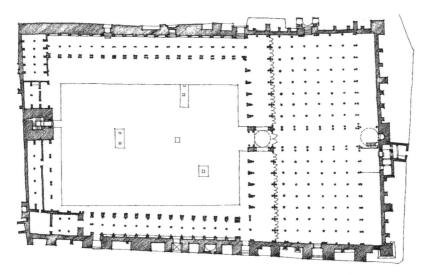

1.10: *Plan, mosque of Sidi 'Uqba ibn Nafi, Kairouan, Tunisia. Drawing © 1995 by Latif Abdulmalik.*

This ornamentation borrows its style from the vegetable world, from geometry, and from epigraphy. The geometrical ornamentation of pagans, Greeks, Christians, and Berbers was extended and refined before being used. Arabic writing, which evolved from simple Kufic, . . . lends itself here to the fantasy of the calligrapher and reveals incomparable quality of decoration. The elements are juxtaposed and mingled to compose a decor.[24]

Sebag's description is not particular to the Kairouan; these elements can be found in other buildings, such as the Great Umayyad mosques at Damascus and Cordoba. What makes this aesthetic language significant is no doubt the unique nature of surface treatment, visual image, epigraphy, and form, which suggests a strong relationship between spatial cognition and belief. The Great Umayyad mosque at Damascus adapts Roman and Byzantine structural columns, which are integrated into the conceptual hierarchical grid of a hypostyle hall.

The significance of this type of juxtaposition is multiple. First and foremost, it presents us with a simulacrum: while the plan of the building is explicit, the use of structural elements is experimental. The use of recycled structural elements at Kairouan and the adaptation of an extant structure at

Damascus legitimized the use of preexisting construction elements. From a theoretical point of view, the ensemble of preexisting structural elements illustrates the borrowing of architectural vocabulary simply for its structural efficacy. However, this newfound architectural expression has contributed to the formation of Islamic art in general.

The process of retrofitting follows a sequence in reverse. For example, the ancient *temenos* (temple of Jupiter Damascenus), which later became the church of St. John the Baptist, was adopted and transformed into a mosque. The key aspect of the transformation was simply the physical orientation of the building to Makkah. The architectural forms of earlier Roman and Byzantine edifices succeeded in expressing a new eclectic language, which reenacted the plan of the Prophet's mosque at Madinah. This unique combination of forms clearly had a significant impact beyond Damascus. Other components in the formation of mosque architecture gained acceptance, since no one thematic or perceptible quality was necessarily symbolic or imposed as a means identification of the faith. Adapted appendages—wall treatment and architectural ornament—do not change the definition of a mosque. At the same time, a number of conventions were rapidly developed during the same general period: the seventh to ninth centuries in Cordoba, North Africa (the Maghrib), and Samara, and after the tenth century in *bilad al-Sudan* (sub-Saharan West Africa).

The cultural transformation of the primordial mosque recognizes the existence of underlying elements, which share a symbiotic relationship with the formation of a vernacular hypostyle. This is more evident in Muslim cultures farther away from the historical nucleus of Islam—for example, in the mosques of China, Malaysia, and West Africa. The West African adaptation of the hypostyle grid plan has been commonly called the Sudanese style. Alan Leary suggests that

> the Mande, and in particular the Dyula whose trading settlements carried the influence of Islam southward from the savannah to the forest verges during the late eleventh and early twelfth centuries, [also carried] the basic forms of the hypostyle mosque design.[25]

Due to the stability and growth of Mande settlements and trading nuclei, the vernacular hypostyle plan became homogeneous within these nuclei.

Because the hypostyle plan is able to sustain and promote architectural variations, a cultural diversity exists in the mosques at Timbuktu, Jenne, and

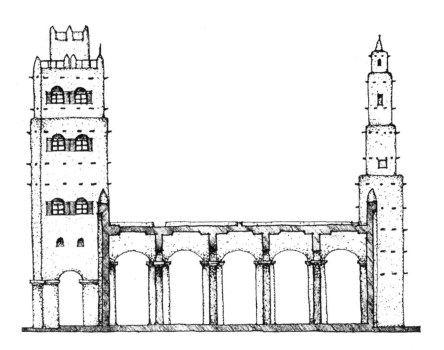

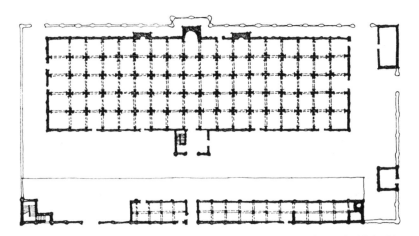

1.11: *Great Mosque of Niono, Mali. Plan and elevation. Drawing © 1995 by Latif Abdulmalik.*

Mopti. Their architectural vocabularies include the repetitive use of pin-
nacles on the roof parapet; the triple minaret on the front façade; and the
buttressing of exterior walls, which produces a vertical exterior rib effect.
The ribs terminate at the parapet and change to decorative crenellations
of varying size. The minarets are always engaged with the building façade,

which is heavily reinforced with structural timber members. The roofs are flat, and the use of domes or vaulted structures is nonexistent in West African mosques (except in the early-nineteenth-century mosques of the Hausa at Kano and Zaria). According to P. F. Stevens, the Dyula (Mande) distinguish three types of mosque.

[T]he *seritongo* used by individuals or small groups of Muslims for daily prayers, is frequently no more than an area of ground marked off by stones. The *misijidi* [*masjid*] or *missiri* or *buru* is used by Muslims from several households or from a Quarter for their daily prayers and for Friday prayers if they have no access to a Friday mosque. The *Jamiu* [*Jum'ah*] or *Missiri-Jamiu* is used for Friday prayers and serves the requirements of the whole *Ummah* [community].[26]

In this way, the Mande mosque shares a functional affinity with the wider community of Islam. While this claim is valid with respect to the liturgical use of a mosque, the Mande mosque remains an aesthetic anomaly. What links the Mande community of artists, blacksmiths, builders, griots, and weavers to a common indigenous tradition are the spatial cognition and the medium of the expression that we find in material culture. Some of the themes are commonly found in the schema of decorative elements of the mosques, which are explicitly expressed but are metaphorically apparent. One example of a metaphorical element is the minaret, which fuses with the *mihrab* to form one element. The *mihrab* bears a close physical association to the baobab tree; examples of this can be seen in the mosques at Bamako, Mali, and at Agades, Niger. The architecture of the granaries on the escarpment of the Bandigara cliffs also corresponds to the structure of the minaret, and like the West African baobab tree, they are sometimes circular but often rectilinear. Kathryn L. Green has suggested another relationship.

The minaret of the mosque would be used as a place for seclusion, a type of cell or *khalwa* which was used for prayer and silence up to a period of seven days. . . . In the [rectilinear] shaped minaret of the Dyula [mosques], a room would be hollowed out to provide a place for seclusion.[27]

It is tempting to suggest a credible relationship between the baobab and the minaret and granary forms, but so far there is no textual or oral evidence that would confirm this relationship, so we can only speak of a meta-

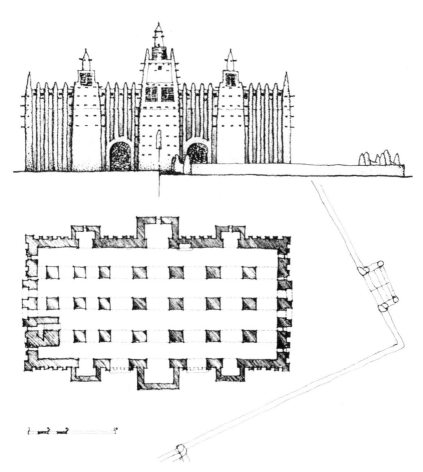

1.12: *Great Mosque of Jenne, Mali. Plan and elevation. Drawing © 1998 by Latif Abdulmalik.*

phorical comparison. With respect to the activities surrounding the formal establishment of Islam in Kong by the Dyla, Green suggests another type of expression, which is both literal and metaphorical in meaning.

> The Mossi ruler from whom Seku Watara seized power [in Kong] had a powerful *djo* [secret sculpture or fetish]. Imam Baro, designated by Seku [Watara] as the leader of the Muslims, buried this fetish and built the large central mosque of Kong over it under the Seku's directions.[28]

The natural environment of the West African savannah lends itself to an ethos of natural existence. The Mande use natural earth to build their mosques, in the same way the Prophet built his mosque at Madinah, and the prescription of not embellishing the building is observed in the Mande mosques as well.[29] It is quite plausible that this is not a coincidence but a conscious act. The absolute simplicity of the Mande building plan cannot be disputed, and in this way it remains faithful to the spatial *sunnah*. Epigraphy is absent from the walls of the edifice; instead, it is the elasticity of earth that gives the façade of the edifice a sculptural form similar to the image one finds in the masking traditions of the region. A sense of beauty is shared between building and object; this idea is realized typically in the façade. Some writers have made serious attempts to depict the Mande mosque as having an imitative relationship with the altars and ancestral pillars found on the West African landscape.[30] They have also suggested that this relationship is deeply rooted in the Mande aesthetic consciousness and that the Mande have implicitly appropriated these forms for the architecture of the mosque. Other writers have even suggested that the syncretic nature of Islam in West Africa has kept pre-Islamic practices alive. Rene Bravmann writes about the masking traditions among the Mande.

> The syncretic nature of Islam in West Africa is based not only on the exigencies of time and place but also on the very makeup of the religion. . . . Masked cults and shrines housing figurative art furnish the means by which the pressing problem of existence can be comprehended and resolved. . . . The acceptance of masking and figurative rituals in an Islamic context therefore cannot be constructed simply as a case of massive back sliding or apostasy, but should be viewed as a reflection of pragmatic results of the confrontation of Islam and traditional cultures.[31]

Bravmann and others follow the line of reasoning propagated by Clifford Geertz and John Spencer Trimingham and many of the French anthropologists working on the Dogon. Among them, the common approach is grounded in structural anthropology, which tries to understand the deep structure through the observation of belief and indigenous religious practice. Failing to understand the deep structure has led many scholars to fall back on notions of totemism and animism. If we consider the state of learning and knowledge of the adherents, this points to a controversy concerning the extent to which vernacular traditions have informed the aesthetics of the mosque.

The Mande mosque is a normative edifice that conforms to the spatial *sunnah*. However, a problem occurs when we begin to deconstruct the non-liturgical elements, to decipher the cultural meanings of elements such as the *mihrab*, the minaret, the façade, and the parapet details. If cities or settlements existed prior to Mansa Musa's fourteenth-century C.E. pilgrimage, then certainly a building tradition existed, as well as builders and their techniques of construction. This theory is further corroborated by the archeological findings of Susan McIntosh and Roderick McIntosh at Jenne and elsewhere in the Sahel.[32]

This discussion has raised more questions than it has answered, but getting to the deep structure of Mande aesthetics demands an exegesis that goes beyond the historical or anthropological path. It demands a process that queries the methodology of form and the decorative genre of vocabulary indigenous to the Mande builders. Archeological studies conducted over the past twenty years have begun to probe the nature of settlement features and the diffusion of building traditions on the Niger bend, primarily at Jenne.[33] These studies show that traditions of both square and round buildings existed in Jenne before 1150 C.E. Jenne was a city or settlement more than thirty hectares in size, with a wall surrounding the city made of cylindrical mud bricks. The technique of building with cylindrical mud bricks is still dominant in Jenne today. In summary, it is clear that further research is needed to formulate conclusive evidence concerning the nature of building activity, trade patterns, and technology among the Mande and, in particular, concerning Mande mosque construction. Various lessons can be drawn from the mosques that were built outside of Madinah from the seventh century onwards and that led to an aesthetic consensus that absorbed vernacular skills and cultural meaning into the construction process.

5. EXPRESSION:
Moorish Aesthetics in America

If we review the numerous sources of Muslim architectural history, we come across an architectural continuum between old and new epochs, between past and present environments. Old and new themes contribute to the genesis of an architectural expression in a new environment. We find examples of the new expression in visual elements and construction devices that were adapted from pre-Islamic civilizations in the lands conquered by Islam. Along with this process of exchange, we find the introduction of visual elements entirely related to conquest in the New World in the fifteenth century, long after the collapse of Muslim dynasties in the Iberian Peninsula. Islamic artistic traditions were introduced to the New World from the initial period of Spanish conquest until the late nineteenth century. These traditions owe their origins to a rich genre of architectural and decorative themes developed in Muslim Spain from the eighth century C.E. until the *reconquista*. By the time the conquistadors began building their churches in the New World, certain Islamic elements had already become an integral part of the Spanish architectural tradition. The arrival of the Spanish missionaries to the New World in the fifteenth century C.E. brought an aggregate of Andalusian styles, infused with secular and religious meaning.[34] For example, the "mission style" in the American Southwest is a theme that is perfectly backed by conquest and a venerable tradition dominated by Christian proselytism. In the mission style, we observe an iteration and rigidifying of new forms but also a friction of forms and materials: a sweeping interchange between Islam and Christianity in the Iberian Peninsula is later translated into the aesthetics of the mission style in the New World. Roger Kennedy explains the translation of architectural forms that were brought from the Maghrib (Algeria, Tunisia, and Morocco) and Andalusia (on the Iberian Peninsula) to the New World.

> The culture of the Muslim Mediterranean was a powerful influence upon the architecture of the Spanish missions in America during the first great building campaign after the conquest. That is why the first Spanish churches created in America look so much like the small mosques of Algeria and Morocco. The churches built by Columbus at La Isabela and by his son Diego at Puerto Real had towers that, in another context, could have been minarets.[35]

Kennedy's view is in general a reasonable one. It recognizes that the mission style has mixed aesthetic affiliations with Islamic architecture. Although the aesthetic traditions of Christianity and Islam have been traditionally separated, conquest in the New World brought a mixed style. The general features of the style are problematic, in that the original use and meaning amount to a new trope or theme. Take for example the term "Moorish style" and its popular use in nineteenth-century architecture in

1.13: *Moorish-style house, Hudson, New York. Photograph © 2000 by Ronald Baker. Courtesy of Ronald Baker.*

America. The aesthetic irony that we find in the use of this style suggests many ambiguities that are attached to the style. We will return to this discussion below.

The *atrio,* or walled-in courtyard, serves as an excellent example of how the extra-muros space of the mission-style complex closely resembles the courtyard space of the North African and Andalusian mosque. George Kubler explains the *atrio* as one of the spatial elements that remained in continuous use.

> Determined by necessity as the form certainly was, one nevertheless may assume that it was partly confined by remote recollections of Moslem congregations, assembled in vast opened courtyards facing the *mihrab,* which gave the direction of Mecca. The problem and the solution are identical in both cases; whether independently invented or affiliated by influence, the Mexican *atrio* follows the expulsion of the Moors by a scant 40 years.[36]

While Christian and Muslim liturgies differ, the *atrio* retained its function as a space for outdoor worship; this practice is clearly related to Muslim worship in the courtyard of the mosque and obviously reflects the immediate influence of Andalusian and North African mosque plans, which always include such courtyards. Even churches with no resident communities retained the use of the *atrio,* where open mass was performed in front of the congregation of Native Americans, who in their own religious traditions were not used to indoor worship.[37] The plan of the mission San Luis Rey de Francia in California is reminiscent of the hypostyle courtyard and plan found in the older mosques in Andalusia and North Africa. However, at San Luis Rey de Francia, the plan is executed with Romanesque arcades.[38] Kennedy admits that the organization of the interior spaces of missions owes its essence to Islam.[39] Referring to the mission San Pedro y San Pablo del Sonora in his chapter "The Horizontality of Mosques and Missions," he describes the edifice as a "façade with mannerist Baroque ornamentation set about a Moorish doorway, and a minaret bell tower."[40] Examples of the *alfiz,* a rectangular label around the horseshoe arch, can be identified in the façade of chapels in Uruapan and Angahuan.[41] The Capilla Real is regarded as the best example of the Moorish style in the Americas. Adjoining a great Gothic church built by Franciscan monks in 1549 in downtown Cholula, it is reminiscent of the mosque of Cordoba, especially in the hypostyle arrangement of columns:

> There are sixty-four columns, forming seven aisles, with a dome over each bay thus formed, hence nearly fifty domes. Some of the columns are round and some are octagonal; and from them round-arches spring, forming pendentives to support the domes. Originally built in the sixteenth century for "overflow" purposes and undoubtedly inspired by the great mosque of Cordoba in Spain, the building collapsed shortly after it was completed and was rebuilt in the seventeenth century.[42]

A reflection of eclecticism emerges when we consider the activity that gave rise to the Moorish styles in the New World, especially the architectural language that resulted in amalgamation of the old and new elements. Spanish Muslims brought the Mudejar style across the Atlantic the same year that Columbus came to America. Later, a second wave of craftsmen fled Spain after the final expulsion of Muslims and Jews in 1609; they were known for their artistry, skill, and workmanship in iron, brass, stone, and wood. On the American mainland, the Mudejar style was later called Spanish or Californian, although it can also be found in Texas, Arizona, Florida, and New Mexico.[43]

The tectonic elements of the Mudejar style have been allowed to continue, but the style has no direct influence on the direction of the contemporary American mosque. What is more, the splendid abstraction of Mudejar art has had no means of entering into harmony with the architecture it evokes and can only be recalled through isolated examples of secular and religious architecture in this hemisphere. In this respect, it is necessary to recall how the Moorish style was adapted in the United States. Since this is not the place for detailed analysis, we will dwell on the general aspects that are strongly reminiscent of Muslim architecture on the Iberian Peninsula prior to 1492.

It may actually be asserted that the Moorish style has subtly eroded since the height of its popularity in nineteenth-century America due to widespread experiments with vaults, arches, and decorated surfaces. We should remember that the starting point of the interest in Moorish architecture was a search by western architects for aesthetic stimulation outside their own time and place. Since the cultural connotations of the style no longer cor-

1.14 (a): *Door detail (arabesque), Dar al-Islam mosque, Abiquiu, New Mexico. Woodwork by Benyamin Van Hattum. Photograph © 1994 by Asad Siddiqui. Courtesy of Asad Siddiqui.*

1.14 (b): *Door detail (arabesque), Dar al-Islam mosque, Abiquiu, New Mexico. Woodwork by Benyamin Van Hattum. Photograph © 1994 by Benyamin Van Hattum. Courtesy of Benyamin Van Hattum.*

responded to a formal expression or essence, its use resulted in a whimsical separation of form and content. The influence of the Moorish style in the United States is still of considerable importance because it was copied in so many instances, assimilated and reproduced more than in any other country in the Western world.

Further aesthetic tensions have been created by the use of the Moorish style, and these tensions have produced visual icons that disorient our sense of time and space. Private villas, public buildings, kiosks, gardens, hotels, expositions, and Jewish synagogues all exhibit marked interpretations of the style, allowing them to express an architect's oriental imagination. For example, architect Henry Austin's work on several villas in New Haven, Connecticut, displays an influence of Islamic motifs in fenestration.[44] Architect William Ranlett's publication of *A Series of Original Designs, 1847-49* describes exotic domes and minarets.[45] Richard Morris Hunt, one of the most celebrated architects of the period, found the Moorish style to be both decorative and appropriate. His cast-iron Islamic motifs received acclaim in both Europe and America. Many American architects took an interest in the "stick style" in the last decades of the nineteenth century; cusped-arches elevations were used in the construction of verandas and porches. The stick style owes its inspiration to the Philadelphia architect Samuel Sloan.[46] In the late nineteenth century, attitudes towards the Moorish style suggested that it had assumed new emphasis, although the demand for aesthetic accuracy had declined. While American architects and builders found the style profoundly enlightening, it was put to use in outright contradiction to conventional definition and description. Buildings such as the New York Crystal Palace, bazaars, markets, and exhibition halls were often decorated with Moorish arches and Islamic tracery, and the interiors of the structures, although oddities, preserved certain decorative elements of the thirteenth-century al-Hambra palace.

Leon A. Jick and others have adequately explained exactly how the Moorish style became an accepted architectural treatment on the Jewish synagogue.[47] One explanation is derived from the fact that Jews and Muslims shared a common architectural legacy in medieval Spain. In the design of the Moorish-style synagogue, Jewish and non-Jewish architects quoted heavily from the influence of medieval Spain, which had already spread to the rest of Europe through the work of architects like Gottfried Semper, Otto Simonson, and Ernst Zwirner. Jewish immigrants from Europe who traveled to America in the nineteenth century apparently brought the style along with them. For example, the B'nai Yeshurun on Plum Street in Cincinnati (1864–1866), designed by James K. Wilson, is principally composed of Moorish elements.[48] It has been described as an "Alhambra temple with slender pillars and thirteen domes."[49] Temple Emanu-El of Fifth Avenue and Forty-third Street in New York (1854; remodeled 1868 by Eidlitz and Fernbac) also firmly incorporated the Moorish style.[50]

Although specific Muslim precedents have been noted in public and domestic buildings, one of the most successful conceptual uses of these elements can be found in the Wainwright tomb (1892) by Louis Sullivan. His inspiration for the tomb's funerary architecture recalled Near Eastern precedents, but it was imitative rather than conceptual.[51] Moorish elements even appear in the work of Frank Lloyd Wright, although these elements are relegated to a secondary role.

We may continue to talk about the use of a unitary aesthetic system in an exotic sense, as Sullivan and others understood it. Clear, binding prescriptions and contradictory aspects of an outdated style led to an aesthetic expression in nineteenth- and early-twentieth-century America. This sense, although externally expressive, did not commit American architects to studying the origins of the style or promoting a critical conversation about the architectural tendencies of another culture. The Moorish style had its own clientele; it corresponded to the needs of a small number of middle-class and conservative clients. It showed itself as a form of technical progress even with its anachronistic constraints.

In the nineteenth century, the problems of a new aesthetic treatment were admittedly tied to new technologies, such as cast iron and industrial production, which were motivated by economic means. Questions were raised regarding the intention of the architect or client. In the same way, we can say the style of the modern mosque remains tied to old symbols and a new technological engagement. In the twentieth century, the attempt to bring the building closer to an alignment with its context—the environment—so that it embodies psychological dimensions of space and time has led to a contextual approach by architects such as Luis Barragán.

Barragán's encounter with the al-Hambra in 1924 exposed him to the subject, style, content, and setting of Moorish architecture. He describes the outcome of his encounter in a way that allows the al-Hambra to serve as a lesson. It is clear that his appreciation is not dulled by artificial understanding of the Moorish style.

> Having walked through a dark and narrow tunnel of the Alhambra,
> I suddenly emerged into the serene, silent solitary *Patios of the Myrtles*
> hidden in the entrails of that ancient palace. Somehow I had the feeling
> that it enclosed what a perfect garden, no matter its size, should enclose—
> nothing less than the entire Universe. This memorable epiphany has
> always been with me, and it is not mere chance that from the first garden
> for which I am responsible all those following are attempts to capture the
> echo of the immense lesson to be derived from the aesthetic wisdom of
> the Spanish Moors.[52]

Barragán's attraction to an earlier age that incorporates different concepts of space and time—Moorish Spain—sustains an interest in Muslim building tradition whose roots can be characterized by relatively circumscribed religious and aesthetic codes. Barragán does not attempt to replicate the "vision of Paradise" that the gardens of the al-Hambra conjure up. Instead, his desire is to capture the meditative quality of the aesthetics, which are effectively religious. The force of this credo shows in the following remarks:

> The greatest impression on my life was a trip I took to Africa. I saw the construction called the Casbah, situated to the south of Morocco. Aesthetically, what I found there is most in harmony with the landscape, the people who live there, their clothing, the atmosphere and even more in tune with their own dances, their families. In other words I found the perfect integration of their religion with the whole environment in which they lived and the material objects with which they came into contact.[53]

As Barragán has noted, the analysis of this aesthetic path redirects his own work in Mexico towards a religious experience, a reorientation that will eventually validate human experience over interpretation, contemplation over rhetoric, and substance over mediocrity.

> It is from the Islamic notion of compartmentalized and successive garden spaces that Barragán developed his feeling for walled enclosures and his love for the sound of running water. . . . Since then Barragán's mind remained attuned to the intimate garden. . . . [I]t is the intimacy of the Islamic garden that seduces him.[54]

The dominant theme in Barragán's aesthetic is context and setting, which are revealed through the dual senses of seeing and hearing. The association between the two is matched by the visual composition of architecture and landscape. In this way, sound is made to fill the time boundaries, just as the repetitive motif of the visual arabesque fills the spatial borders in incessant movement.

A serious criticism concerns the primacy given to widespread use of the Moorish style in America without proper knowledge of methods for combining the vocal with the visual. In the absence of this knowledge, the style remains emotionally satisfying, but it excludes all of the spiritual associations that are so crucial to any culture's underlying belief system. Although the Moorish style enjoyed popular consensus in America, the outcome is for the most part cosmetic; the use of the style is dubious. It does not promote a deep understanding, which is necessary for the development of an architectural production. It would be too easy and too cursory to consider the Moorish style a design criterion for the American mosque despite its presence in the New World for over three hundred years. Rather, in designing the American mosque, a complex new set of problems faces the architect and the client: (1) each new mosque has its own aesthetic program that is the result of either a historic, a cultural, or an ethnic perspective; and (2) each program can be analyzed as a process of cultural and religious production and as a reflection of tradition or future prospects. These difficulties will not be overcome simply by falling back on traditional conventions or stylistic apparatus, even if the temptation to do so may appear legitimate.

INTERPRETATIONS OF IMAGE, TEXT, AND FORM

Chapter Two

1. AESTHETIC COMPLEXITIES:
The Appearance of the American Mosque

The aesthetic features of the American mosque can be codified under the rubrics of "image," "text," and "form."[1] These three features suggest an anachronistic language corresponding to the use of ornament, inscription, and architectural form. The occurrence of image, text, and form, therefore, prompts an inquiry that must address two pivotal thematic assumptions:

1. The primacy of prayer (*salat*) is a necessary criterion in determining the characteristics of a liturgical space suited for the American environment.[2]
2. The embellishment of a space for *salat* is a contingent matter. Although ornament, inscription, and architectural form have been nuanced as integral aspects of the aesthetic language of a mosque, these features are essentially independent of any ritual demands.

Both assumptions provide the scope to study the aesthetic language of the American mosque with regard to the complexities of ornament, inscription, and architectural form. But we encounter, with regard to the second assumption, a recurring use of an extant aesthetic precedent. In the history of Muslim architecture, we come upon instances in which the aesthetic features of an extant mosque have influenced a succeeding structure. There are exceptions to the foregoing premise, and the question of the degree to which an extant mosque can be considered in the classification of the American mosque is further complicated by the absence of documented

2.1: *Islamic Center of Greater Toledo, Toledo, Ohio. Photograph © 1996 by Daud Abdul-Aziz. Courtesy of Daud Abdul-Aziz.*

history.[3] In addition, the features of the American mosque appear to be directly related to the phenomenon of a Muslim diaspora. When building a mosque, the diaspora community ascribes emotional value to the utilization of a well-known convention or an influencing custom from the Muslim world. The history of Muslim architecture is, therefore, a key consideration for an architect who aims to gratify a Muslim client. However, there are problems with the indiscriminate use of a well-known convention or an influencing custom. In attempting to replicate extant features from the past, the architect invariably produces a de facto facsimile whose aesthetics are severely compromised. For example, truckers were overheard commenting on their shortwave radios as they drove past the mosque in Toledo, Ohio, which was under construction at the time. One trucker, responding to his friend who had asked him about the structure of the mosque, remarked that "it must be a new Mexican restaurant or something"![4]

We may forgive the naïveté of the trucker inasmuch as he is not expected to recognize the appearance of a *masjid*. His comment, however, reinforces the following point: In our inquiry, the aesthetic features of an American mosque must be thoughtfully examined with respect to the idiosyncratic treatment and usage of image, text, and form. The discourse that follows attempts to do just that.

The first debate that we must address examines the heterogeneous use of image. In the American mosque, image is appropriated in an anachronistic manner; it is used as a display of ornament without regard to time or context. Image is essentially concerned with satisfying an emotional condition that has historical efficacy for the immigrant Muslim community. The appropriation of a familiar image vividly evokes a mental picture or an apparition that closely resembles an extant form, object, or likeness emanating from the past.[5]

The second debate examines the appropriation of form. Architects have reinterpreted multiple geometric forms and spatial elements found in various extant models and decorative conventions. The intent is to produce a new aesthetic language that will be appropriate to the American environment. Inasmuch as the interpretation of form falls under the purview of the architect, the divergent ways in which architects have interpreted the architectural features of an extant model or decorative convention make an intriguing study. It should be noted that the attributes of form are distinct from those associated with image. Unlike image, form is concerned with the ordering of a design program for a mosque and the production of a coherent site condition. The interpretation of form is further complicated by the nuances of American architectural practice. For instance, architectural pedagogy considers form to be the shape, structure, and pattern of an object, or the secular mode in which an object exists, acts, and manifests itself by derivation and by composition.[6]

The third debate examines the use of epigraphy; it concerns the treatment of textual inscriptions in a mosque. Because textual inscriptions have customarily been sanctioned in religious buildings in the Muslim world, it is an aesthetic convention that appeals to the diaspora community as well. The use of epigraphy is further complicated by the fact that the linguistic makeup of the American congregation is very different from that of congregations in other parts of the world: most American Muslims do not speak Arabic. Hence, the utilization of Arabic inscriptions in an American mosque raises several issues: Is the purpose of a pious inscription to evoke a symbolic charge—a term I borrow from Professor Oleg Grabar—or is it intended to be decorative, a means to enhance the image of a structure or merely to adorn a wall? Who reads the text of the inscription? Would a mosque with a pious inscription be more reverent than a *masjid* lacking an inscription?

These issues are all equally provocative and deserve further discussion, for they are relevant to the ensuing discourse. I will return to them.

An overriding debate deals with the production of an image. Within a climate of uncommon architectural language, where extremes of architectural diversity exist, the meaning of an image can only be fostered through use of one or more aspects of a known architectural convention. Since the immigrant community views Muslim religious architecture as clearly more homogeneous than Western architecture, the use of a known architectural convention takes precedent. I would, however, hasten to add that the study of art and architecture anywhere, or indigenous to any culture, is cognizant of internal variations and aesthetic complexities.[7]

By reanimating an image from the past, the first generation of Muslim immigrants from the Middle East and the Indian subcontinent has held firmly to the production of a recognizable religious image.[8] The utilization of a religious image gives outward expression and meaning to the presence of an Islamic practice in North America.[9] In addition to providing a place for communal worship, a mosque with a recognizable image imparts identity and also produces an emotional charge. Emotions and sentiments are thus evoked through the agency of memory; despite geographical, historical, and chronological nuances, the features of an extant image, when reanimated, become a common aesthetic ethos, and the image is happily embraced by the community.[10] By recalling an image from the past, one no longer remains in an alien environment but becomes part of an environment where belief and emotions are nourished by familiar aesthetic themes.

The decision to use or not to use inscription as part of the design vocabulary of an American mosque entails several unique problems. First, one must evaluate the symbolic value of an inscription. Second, the functional intent within the overall design concept of a mosque must also be considered. Mosques in America have de-emphasized the use of inscriptions, but perhaps the reason is a very practical one: skilled calligraphers are not easily found within the American Muslim community. However, the use of inscriptions also raises some religious concerns: Would a worshipper—who may not be able to read the text—be more concerned with the decorative quality of the inscription or with the spiritual charge it emits? Would the space for prayer be enhanced by the presence of an inscription?

The fact that such a large community of non-Arabic-speaking Muslims resides in America raises the question of whether inscriptions are necessary at all. Whether to use inscriptions or not is a matter that, in the end, each individual community must decide for itself. If we consider the premise of a precedent as a decisive criterion, we could argue that inscriptions are not used in many instances.[11] Both the designer and the client may be persuaded by an imitative approach, in which case inscriptions are significant for the purpose of satisfying an emotional condition. Alternately, the designer who takes an entirely rational approach would find that inscriptions are less significant and may even be viewed as extraneous to a mosque's overall aesthetic condition.

Three crucial questions remain unanswered with respect to the composite use of aesthetics found in extant models.

1. Can a contemporary architect design a mosque that expresses the idiomatic qualities inherent in the composite features of an extant model?
2. How does the architect define what the expressive qualities of an extant model actually are?[12]
3. Is it possible to achieve visual affinity with an extant model without hyperrationality or blatant mediocrity?[13]

In framing these three questions in a discourse, and with regard to image, text, and form, it becomes evident that the aesthetic language of the American mosque remains an enigma. I would like to conclude with some tentative considerations about the complexities of the enigma surrounding the subject of historical continuity and the primacy of 'ibadah (acts of worship or ritual). In taking into account the complexities of the enigma, we must consider the two assumptions made at the beginning of this essay. The first assumption postulates the primacy of salat (prayer) as a necessary criterion in studying the characteristics of a devotional space. It regards salat as the essence of 'ibadah, and it is summed up in a much-quoted phrase from the Prophet Muhammad: "The [whole] earth is a masjid for you, so wherever you are at the time of prayer, make your prostration there."[14]

Viewed in terms of historical continuity, the American mosque finds its expression in a valued origin with an affinity to the first mosque at Madinah (seventh century c.e.). The development of the first prototype and its later aesthetic expressions was sustained via a commonly understood cosmological order.[15] The Muslim cosmological order can be defined by five ordering themes: belief, order, space, materials, and symbols.[16] These ordering themes find their primordial origin in the Madinah mosque, which was originally a simple, demarcated, orthogonal, walled space, with an open courtyard with

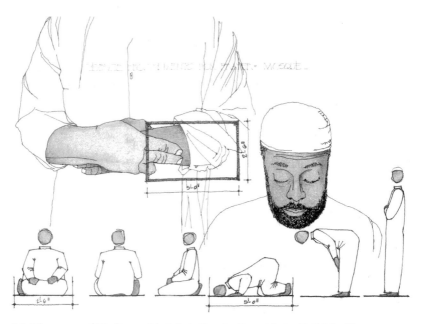

2.2: *The postures of Muslim worship* (*salat*)*. Drawing © 1998 by Latif Abdulmalik.*

two or three doors and, at one end, a shaded, rectangular portico (*musallah*) facing Makkah.[17] Rational sciences were engaged as means of demonstrating the idiosyncratic aesthetic themes and a holistic architectural expression, in view of belief, order, space, materials, and symbols.[18] In the development of the American mosque, the use of rational science as an ordering device has not been an end in itself, and therefore, the driving force of historical continuity in terms of image, text, and form must also be taken into account.

2. A SYNCRETIC IMAGE:
The Islamic Cultural Center, Washington, D.C.

Familiar aesthetic themes are evident in the first major congregational masjid constructed in North America, in Washington, D.C.[19] In selecting the model and aesthetic image for the *masjid,* the client turned toward fifteenth-century Mamluk Egypt.[20] The mosque was designed by Mario Rossi, an Italian architect, who had designed several buildings of this type in Alexandria and Cairo between 1940 and 1950.[21] He designed the Washington mosque using what can be called a neo-Mamluk vocabulary. The resulting image discloses the geographical origins of Rossi's clients. The principal client was a Palestinian Muslim, but the financial sponsors of the building were several Muslim ambassadors from the Middle East, Turkey, and the Indian subcontinent who were assigned to Washington, D.C. By recalling the past, Rossi's design for the mosque makes a statement about memory and image in two principal ways. First, it ignores the American architectural context; it makes no effort to address the prevailing architectural language or the sense of place. Second, it reinforces memory by using traditional crafts and calligraphy that were imported from Turkey, Iran, and Egypt, along with the craftsmen whose skills were engaged in the decoration of the mosque.[22]

The plan of the building is a three-*iwan* hall framed by an exterior double-*riwaq* arcade, which serves as an extra-muros space, or *ziyadah*. The orthogonal arcade remains perpendicular to the street, but the mosque is set out at a tangent to conform to the *qiblah* axis, which was calculated using the great circle, or the shortest distance to Makkah.[23] In Mamluk buildings, there would be a *sahn,* or courtyard, open to the sky, that shared a contiguous space with the *iwans*; but owing to climatic reasons, the whole central space of the mosque is covered with a modest clerestory dome. A *riwaq* (hypostyle hall), consisting of five contiguous Andalusian arches (perhaps symbolic of the five pillars of faith), defines the façade and serves as an entry portal. The *riwaq* is yet another anomaly; Andalusian arches are not to be found in Mamluk buildings.

The entry portal runs parallel to the street, and for added emphasis, it is recognized by an inscription band of neo-Kufic script at the upper part of the façade, which reads, "In houses of worship which Allah has permitted to be raised so that His name be remembered, in them, there [are such as] extol His limitless glory at morning and evening" (Q. 24:36). Several verses of the Qur'an have been arranged in a symmetrical configuration and in various patterns on the interior walls and ceilings of the mosque. The divine names of Allah (*asma' Allah al-Husna*) and several familiar and often quoted verses from the Qur'an (such as Q. 96:1–5) are inscribed in large framed borders of Thuluth (one of the six major styles of calligraphy), along with smaller framed panels of ornamental Kufic script.[24]

Two inscription bands run horizontally across the face of the *mihrab*. The one at the top reads, "Verily we have seen the turning of your face to the heaven, . . ." and the lower band, just slightly higher than a man's height, continues, ". . . surely we shall turn you to a *qiblah* that shall please you"

2.3: *Islamic Cultural Center of Washington, Washington, D.C. Muhammad Rossi, architect. Photograph © 1999 by Talha Sarac. Courtesy of Talha Sarac.*

2.4: *Islamic Cultural Center of Washington, Washington, D.C. Muhammad Rossi, architect. Photograph © 1999 by Talha Sarac. Courtesy of Talha Sarac.*

(Q. 2:144). The *mihrab* is a hybrid element: its decorative treatment follows the Iznik and Bursa tradition of using glazed tiles—blue, red, and green—which are commonly found in Ottoman buildings.

The mosque's composition epitomizes an array of Muslim aesthetic themes. The overall image that the inscriptions evoke is, in regard to the use of epigraphy, significant in two ways: first as a devotional theme, and second as an emotional device. While the symbolic meaning of the inscriptions would satisfy a worshiper with a quiet, devotional disposition, the *masjid*'s form evokes the image of a Mamluk prototype that has been reanimated from the fifteenth century C.E.

The evocative appeal of Rossi's neo-Mamluk edifice is telling. The building's artful use of authentic motifs that can be traced back to an earlier epoch reminds observers of the past. More disturbing, however, is the fact that architecture is used as a resource to establish continuity with the past. This concept is not a new one, yet the potential danger inherent in trying to replicate an extant image is significant for an innocent eye. In this sense, Rossi was either consciously or unconsciously manipulating time, even though the context is comparatively a new one. American architect Robert Venturi adopted a similar approach in his design proposal for the Baghdad State

Mosque. Art historians and architects might approve or disapprove of Rossi's and Venturi's ideas, but the larger question concerns the use of architecture to evoke a vivid sense of the past; the result is met with either praise or reproach. Clearly, in the composition of the Washington mosque, Rossi felt free to mix and match, to use a variety of forms to create a new composition, even though the original meanings of the forms are absent. The edifice provokes an even deeper question about meaning and origin. Undoubtedly, the building reflects an embodiment of cultural nuances that are meaningful to the client, which validates the interdependence of the past and the present. In this sense, the past is the present, and therefore it could be argued that

> Everything must have an antecedent; nothing in any genre comes from nothing and this may apply to all man's creations and inventions. In spite of the subsequent changes *in time and place,* all things have conserved visibly and in a way evident to feelings and to reason this elementary principle, which is like a nucleus that collects and coordinates in time the variations of form. In this way we have achieved a thousand things in each genre, and one of the principal occupations of science and philosophy is to understand the reasons for them and to discover their origin and primitive cause.[25]

Art is not created ex nihilo, so we need hardly point out the emotional impetus and nostalgic sentiment of the clients—all of whom were émigrés to the United States or foreign diplomats. Invoking the past as a reminder of their origins allowed for two types of reflection that are not always evident in human emotions and reason: (1) the edifice provided sentimental aesthetic substance and functioned as a nucleus, a familiar place to gather; and (2) it gave the client and end user a sense of religious and cultural identity in an alien North American environment.

3. AN AVANT-GARDE EXPRESSION:
The Islamic Cultural Center of New York, Manhattan, New York

The production of a building that mimics an extant prototype demands traditional workmanship, materials, and skills, all of which are not readily available in the United States. Moving away from a strictly traditional approach, the designers of the Manhattan *masjid* have explored the use of modern technology as a compositional device without limitation. The Manhattan *masjid* confronts the issue of tradition *versus* modernity by seeking to reinterpret various aesthetic themes associated with an extant model found in the Muslim world.[26] There are several observations to be made in this regard. First, the surface motifs reflect geometric themes, which are employed as a unifying element throughout the mosque's interior and exterior. The geometric motifs bear a close resemblance to Piet Mondrian's paintings, particularly his *Broadway Boogie Woogie*. These motifs can be seen primarily on the carpet where worshippers assemble for prayer in parallel, horizontal rows facing the *qiblah*. They also appear in the surface treatment of the *minbar* (rostrum, podium, pulpit), in the exterior façade, and in several other interior elements. Geometry is a fundamental theme in Muslim cosmology, but in this case, it comes closer to a modernist, secular interpretation than to a traditional, cosmological one.

The inscriptions included in the decorative features of the *masjid*'s interior are rendered in a geometric Kufic style. They are set in straight horizontal and vertical arrangements, which accommodate a modernist concept of order. For instance, around the *mihrab,* the geometric Kufic script reads, "Allah is the Light of the heavens and the earth" (Q. 24:35). The text is composed so as not to corrupt the *mihrab*'s geometric themes, which would have been frenzied by a stylized script such as Thuluth.[27] A stylized Thuluth or a floral version of Kufic script would have been in disharmony with the overall modernist composition and surface treatment. The modernist interpretation and its resulting aesthetic image raise the question of whether the mosque's composition has positively achieved a desired aesthetic balance using epigraphic and geometric themes.

Admittedly, the use of traditional inscriptions as a decorative element is in some respects incongruent with the idea of a secular, modernist interpretation of surface treatment. Using geometry as a spatial theme, aided by a correspondingly angular Kufic inscription, produces a visual affinity; a less complementary script would have put the theme of composition and order at risk. The aesthetic treatment of the interior of the dome over the central prayer hall further illustrates this last point. The dome's structural ribs have been left bare and rudimentary, providing a bold geometric texture to the dome's inner face when seen from below. The inner drum of the dome is

2.5 and 2.6: *Islamic Cultural Center of New York, Manhattan, New York. Skidmore Owings and Merrill, architect. Photographs © 1999 by Birol Furat. Courtesy of Birol Furat.*

covered with a band of angular Kufic inscription, but the pattern of concentric ribs clearly dominates the composition, especially since the text of the band is largely unreadable from the main prayer hall below. Both compositional elements—epigraphy and geometry—were clearly intended by the architect to be operative aesthetic devices and to have, in addition, a specific religious character and image, connected to text and form.

This rudimentary analysis shows how SOM, the designer of the New York mosque, made it possible to give a completely different architectural definition to an extant architectural style by testing various design assumptions and engaging in historical interpretation. As far as historical interpretation is concerned, we may ask a crucial question: Is the history of Islamic architecture a pure history? To answer this question, it is important to consider two aspects of the New York mosque's composition: the theoretical and the empirical. By doing so, it will be possible to explain how design assumptions work and how the functional content relates to the aesthetic content. Since both aspects are equally valid but not synonymous, they may suggest a new direction of design. This new approach to understanding the architecture of an American mosque appears to be the one that SOM chose.

The architects were capable of developing an independent, avant-garde expression, and there are reasons why such an expression is not inherently alien to traditional aesthetics. First, it is perfectly legitimate to take this approach and to arrive at an innovative expression, since Islam is not antithetical to reason or innovation. Conceiving architecture in this way invokes the use of the legal term "*ijtihad,*" or independent reasoning. A theoretical elaboration of *ijtihad* with reference to architecture, urbanism, and legal judgment requires an entirely different discussion, which is outside the purview of this essay. However, as far as the design of a contemporary *masjid* is concerned, we must keep in mind three guiding principles: order, habitat, and repose.

Second, the use of architectural innovation—when substituted by the term "modernity"—is clearly justified to meet the needs of the immediate community. This principle is parallel to the concept of public interest, or *maslahah* in Maliki law. We will consider in further detail the concepts of *maslahah, ijtihad,* and legal judgment in chapter 3. Apart from the concept of *maslahah,* it is foolish to speak of material, embellishment, form, and space as distinct parts of the edifice, independent of individual experience and spatial cognition.

If we observe the formative themes (which establish the principles of design), order, habitat, and repose are engaged in the New York mosque, so the value of modernity need not violate any religious principle. Whether or not the novelty of modernity is the only criterion for a contemporary mosque is perhaps debatable. The corollary of this argument is that a building tradition should only be modified if the needs of the community make it necessary or essential. This view prevails in some sectors of the community today, so it is always a source of discontent.

Third, there are convincing reasons to endorse the innovative approach taken by SOM, since form and space can be adapted to novel uses that serve the purpose of the community. Nevertheless, the problem of defining which aspects of form and space are traditional and which are modern—while including the legal aspect of religious practice—has led to dissenting opinions. These opinions would seem not to have any legal footing, since the problem of architectural judgment has very little relevance to religious practice, and since the physical requirements of a mosque are largely the outcome of community consensus (*ijma*). Evidence of dissent can be found in the case of the New York mosque in spite of the cosmopolitan makeup of the New York City community. The project designer, Michael McCarthy, admits that he received advice throughout the planning process from two groups:

> One group urged on him virtually total freedom in the use of forms and motifs, consistent with general respect for Islamic beliefs and architectural tradition. The second group sought literal versions of historic motifs. McCarthy chose to follow the first path. He justified this decision by pointing out that Islam, in its vast conquests, absorbed the best of local building techniques and materials under an overall umbrella of careful geometric ordering of mass, enclosure and finishes.[28]

Clearly, the project designer exercised independent aesthetic judgment in the reworking of extant models from the past. The building takes on additional resonance that reveals the designer's reasoning and the subtlety of his interpretation. Yet notwithstanding the real capacity of aesthetics to be evocative and provocative, the aesthetic language is daringly analytical, fresh, engaging, and free. It is textured with simple reminders of the past and a curious mixture of metaphors, which produce a decidedly marked effect. Specifically, as McCarthy explains, the attempt to recover some notion of the spirit of Islam prevails in the careful use of geometric ordering, mass, enclosure, and finishes. Even here, the design intent lies not so much in a literal interpretation of these elements, but in McCarthy's own attempt to revisit the transporting power of architecture—apropos to place and time, which are conditions that any designer will find difficult. Finally, in terms of design criteria, it is always possible to question the economic base of the undertaking and how far this has determined the outcome of the project.

No one would argue that SOM's avant-garde conception of religious aesthetics has emerged as the dominant one today. For one thing, there is still the tendency for the aesthetics of the American mosque to collapse into a theological argument. Instead of contemplating the distinction between theology and religious practice, as well as the value of order, habitat, and the building's performance, many clients and architects rely on a literal interpretation. The view of religious aesthetics presented by SOM in the New York *masjid* accords with the inclination towards independent reasoning (*ijtihad*), which may suggest a high degree of conceptual interpretation.

Luckily, it includes the interest of the community and does not ignore the uniqueness of aesthetic creation or the understanding of order, habitat, and repose.

4. A TRANSCENDENT FORM:
The Islamic Center of Plainfield, Plainfield, Indiana

Can an American mosque redefine the geometric themes found in Islamic cosmological patterns, such as trajectory (*ramy*), line (*khatt*), balance (*ilmam*), and posture (*isbah*)? In our next example, the architect's interpretation of these ordering themes represents an introspective (*batin*) definition of the essence of geometry that aims to obtain a rich set of aesthetic ideas that are thematic, cosmological, and nondecorative. The mosque of the Islamic Society of North America at Plainfield, Indiana, was designed by Professor Gulzar Haider.[29] The operational scheme of the edifice reinterprets the square, which is repeatedly rotated along the longitudinal trajectory (*ramy*) of the plan. It is anchored to one end of the plan in the form of a mosque. The mosque itself is a set of vertically juxtaposed squares. On the opposite end of the plan, a much larger pattern of the same theme houses administrative and ancillary services. When geometric elements of the square are juxtaposed, a set of very interesting additive and repetitive spatial cores is created. In this scheme, the multi-unit geometric themes employed relate to a two-tiered order: first, their essence and esoteric structure (*batini*), and second, their external appearance (*zahiri*). There is no attempt to diffuse the hierarchies of spaces that emerge as a result of juxtaposition. Geometry is central to the design of the building, to the extent that Qur'anic inscriptions have been de-emphasized. Unlike in the Manhattan mosque, where the inscriptions are present as a decorative agent, in Professor Haider's scheme, decoration is disassociated in order to allow the essence and primacy of geometry to dominate. By emphasizing the elements of a cosmological geometric form and de-emphasizing text, the architect has achieved a desired balance that considers the use of technology suited to the efficacy of American construction methods. The scheme achieves this balance without having to compromise the spirit of the extant tradition of using geometry as an ordering principle.[30]

The use of geometry as a thematic principle may have implications with

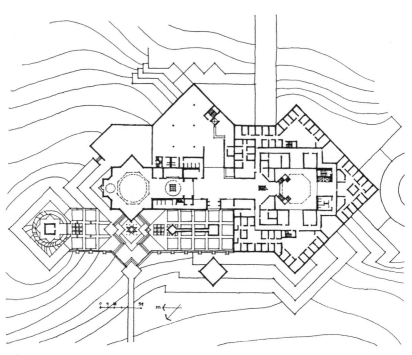

2.7: *Master plan, Islamic Center of Plainfield, Plainfield, Indiana. Gulzar Haider, architect. Drawing prepared by Latif Abdulmalik after Gulzar Haider.*

regard to discrepancies between the use of technology and the American method of construction. However, Haider's appeal to reason and experience in terms of what he calls the guiding principles for architecture in a non-Islamic environment is seriously challenging. Geometry promotes the organization of a spatial pattern and the hierarchy of symbolic elements that are in spatial equilibrium. Haider discourages the use of imitative forms, and he encourages a design program that emphasizes a cognition of the mosque in the American environment. Haider's theory stands as an example of what we have discussed earlier with regard to the use of the historical past as a kind of aesthetic continuum. What makes his theory important is the fact that Haider understands the problem of architecture for Muslim communities in those parts of the world that are "ideologically, culturally and historically non-Islamic."[31] His theory becomes exceptionally plain in the following remarks:

> Most of us cherish and take great joy in history. However, it is important that our past-anchored thinking be replaced by some anticipatory and

visionary thought. We may construct, though not necessarily physically, some utopian models of Islamic reality for discussion and debate. If we start from a utopian construct and tenaciously stay as close to it as possible, while bringing it down to match the present reality, we will get better architecture than if our starting point were the highly constrained and pragmatism-ridden present reality.[32]

It is not so much that Haider's argument sums up the dichotomy between reality and myth, between east and west, and between the past and the present; rather, his remarks indicate that there is value in extant Islamic models. If we take the mosque, then any regional model may present an example of noble endurance—but perhaps nowhere has the example of the mosque been extended to such an extreme as in the West. If there is to be a design rationale for an American mosque, it is also necessary that the designer understand history in order to demonstrate an intelligent solution. Not only is there a modern tendency among architects to consider the past as either thematic or mimetic, but very little attempt is made to distinguish between simplicity and originality in the form of good or bad structures—hence the present complexity of imitation or some other representational tendency in architecture today. It would seem then that the defining character of the American mosque is not a choice between idea and form but rather a conjunction of the two and, as Haider would argue, a dynamic proportion of meaning and object.

In setting out the design principles for the Indiana mosque, Haider describes several design conditions, which indicate the deficiency of one aesthetic view and the strengths of another. He also indicates ways to enhance the design, character, and function of a religious edifice in a non-Islamic environment, where it will ultimately appear as a dichotomy between meaning and mimesis. Some of these techniques are as follows:

- [The architecture must express] unity as its existence: one God, one truth, one existence.
- [The architecture must express] Qur'an as its message.
- [The architecture must express] prophetic tradition and Islamic law as its path: the framework for functional programming.
- The [s]tructure and form of religious activities such as ablution, prayer, and Friday congregation should be treated with utmost care, and preserved and reinforced by architecture.

- The sacred and the [m]undane are to be integrated through continuity and juxtaposition, yet differentiated by the character of space and form. For example, architecture should ensure that it is an act of conscious will to step inside a mosque, as compared to (for example) walking from the library stacks to the reading area.
- Th[e] architecture should be expressive and understandable to all. It should employ a form language [that] for the immigrant Muslims evokes a sense of belonging in their present *environment* and hope in their future. To indigenous Muslims it should represent a linkage with Muslims from other parts of the world, and should underscore the universality and unity of Islam. To non-Muslims it should take the form of clearly identifiable buildings [that] are inviting and open, or at least not secretive, closed [or] forbidding.
- [The architecture] should exhibit a sense of economy of architectural means and generosity of Islamic-humanistic ends. There should be nothing, whether functional or symbolic, without a purpose. It should not be temperamental nor . . . capricious architecture.
- [The architecture] should be ecologically appropriate; embellished and reinforced [by] the natural context; . . . energy-conserving and climatically sensible.
- [The architecture] should be technologically appropriate in terms of the choice of materials and techniques of construction.
- In the choice of architectural motifs [the design] should in no way reinforce the erroneous mythology of Near Eastern "Islamic" exotica [such as that found in] *The Thousand and One Nights*.[33]

Haider's design conditions involve symbolic interpretation and an analogy with design thinking that seeks to find the essence of aesthetic expression. There are certain parallels in this search with intelligible beauty and an allegorical meaning. Perhaps the best account for this interpretation is to be found in the following remarks.

All things visible, when they obviously speak to us symbolically, that is when they are interpreted figuratively, are referable to invisible significations and statements. . . . For since their beauty consists in the visible forms of things . . . visible beauty is an image of invisible beauty.[34]

2.8 (a–d): *Islamic Center, Plainfield, Indiana. Gulzar Haider, architect. Photographs © 1997 by Akel Ismail Kahera.*

5. A SIMPLE ORDER:
Dar Al-Islam Village, Abiquiu, New Mexico

In 1980, the late Hassan Fathy (d. 1989) was commissioned to design and build a mosque and to prepare the master plan for a traditional Muslim village, Dar al-Islam, at Abiquiu, New Mexico. The mesa site is framed by surrounding arid hills and several snow-capped mountains that are visible in the distance. The site at Abiquiu is accessible via a five-mile unpaved country road, which climbs the mesa. At the top, one can expect to experience the reflective aura of the mosque and the *madrasah* upon entering the contemplative silence of the rooms.[35]

2.9: *Dar al-Islam mosque, Abiquiu, New Mexico. Hassan Fathy, architect. Photograph © 2000 by Ronald Baker. Courtesy of Ronald Baker.*

Abiquiu, the Charma River valley, and their immediate surroundings were populated before the arrival of the Spanish by several Native American peoples: Anasazi, Tew, Navajo, Ute, Comanche, Apache, and Genizoro, who were mainly from the pueblos of Hopi, Zuni, Isleta, and Santa Clara. Spanish settlers arrived in 1598 and continued settling in the area until the eighteenth century. The harsh environmental conditions at Abiquiu provided an ideal setting for the widespread *Los Hermanos de la Luz,* the Christian Penitente Brotherhood, which was embraced by the Spanish settlers.

The Dar al-Islam (Abode of Islam) village was the dream of an American-born Muslim and an American-educated Saudi industrialist who met at Makkah in the late 1970s. The original idea was to establish a Muslim village, the largest and most comprehensive of its kind in America.[36] Today the Dar al-Islam organization emphasizes education first, and the site provides a quiet retreat for programs for American educators, Muslims, and non-Muslims. Current activities include secondary teacher training, Muslim Powwow (a gathering of Muslims with cultural roots), and Deen Intensives (intensive training in traditional Islamic sciences for Muslims).

Fathy's mosque and its ancillary buildings undoubtedly belong to the site; they propose a clean, demarcated space for worship facing Makkah. The traditional adobe technique worked well for the choice of site and the project itself. There are no major design anomalies, but the concept raises some questions concerning the design principles, which can be applied elsewhere in North America. Fathy's work is controversial because his architecture remains largely philosophical, hence largely misread. His philosophical ideas present a non-Western tradition; he and Rossi are the only two non-resident Muslim architects who have built major projects in North America. Fathy came to Abiquiu during the initial period of construction. By using adobe construction, Fathy remained faithful to his tectonic tradition, employing a natural material that implicitly endorses the notion of "small is beautiful." As Fathy puts it,

> Tradition is a key element of culture, when the craftsman was responsible for much of the work of building, traditional art came out of the subconscious of the community. . . . On the other hand, the modern architect comes out of the conscious mind of the individual architect. . . . The village built by accretion is more harmonious than the one built on the drawing board; it is held together by an accumulated culture, rather than by one individual's idea of harmony.[37]

The Abiquiu site shares an empathic relationship with Fathy's theory of creativity: human orientation, inward and outward correlation of intimate spaces, and above all, a natural form that blends with the landscape. Fathy's balanced spiritual awareness of a sense of unity among building, landscape, and user imposes an intangible order on the building and the site. According to Fathy,

> In this ever-changing world of things, man is in need of relating himself to some fixed point of reference to get out of chaos into cosmos. He has ever been seeking to situate himself in space, time and the world of the spirit and the mind. . . . In the world of the spirit and the mind, he has been looking for what is immutable within change beyond the material form of truth, having recourse to the three tributaries of knowledge, intuition and faith, philosophy and science. . . . The revealed knowledge of the sage is now replaced with the modern analytical sciences, while the skill of the craftsman's hand has been replaced by the machine. . . . The architect has to remember that wisdom does not belong to a unique epoch, it belongs to all times. It is present today as it was yesterday, and can be realized by anyone who desires it and who deserves it. Nowadays

the procedure and methods of design and building have changed from sufi master craftsman to the architect-contractor system in which design and execution of the work are split, and the canons of sacred art are lost.[38]

It is because of the foregoing remarks that Hassan Fathy's architecture has been completely misread; Fathy's mention of a "sufi master craftsman" points to a tradition of existence that acknowledges divine intervention in all aspects of human affairs, including architecture. Fathy sees himself as merely an individual incidental to his work; at New Mexico and earlier at Gourna, his tectonic style has revived the memory of building traditions that were lost or forgotten. At New Mexico, Fathy brought nothing new to architecture; his reasoning for the mosque and the Abiquiu site is a reaffirmation of preexisting building traditions. Tradition in this sense invokes knowledge of the past, which transcends spatio-temporal categories or labels.

I would like to suggest another way to understand Fathy's work. Intrinsic in the Muslim notion of being is the concept of self pertaining to the confines of the body. In the Occident, the skin and clothing indicate the boundary of self; in the Orient, the concept of self is associated with an essence that lies deep within the body: the soul. Likewise, the essence of the traditional Muslim house is not the façade but the courtyard. Titus Burckhardt suggests that the courtyard or inner sanctuary of a Muslim house is analogous to the *hijab,* the veil worn by Muslim women.[39] The Qur'an prescribes the veil for women; in response to this injunction, the Muslim woman conceals in public various parts of her body that she is permitted to reveal in private to her husband or close kin.

Similarly, there exists in Muslim architecture a tradition that is tied to respect for privacy and public conduct, and it is reflected in the way a house is arranged between the private and the public realms. Burkhardt's concept of that which is concealed (*batin*) or revealed (*zahir*) indicates a greater notion of existence that drives certain questions: Can architecture remind us of the divine presence? Since architecture is a manifestation of temporal existence, is it able to provide life itself with meaning? The sufi master builders understood the notion of existence that was reflected in the spatial and decorative themes of a building.

Fathy's architecture depicts an association with *fitrah:* natural tendency, innate character, temperament, or natural disposition; truth and order. These terms confer a definition of existence that is entirely apart from Vit-

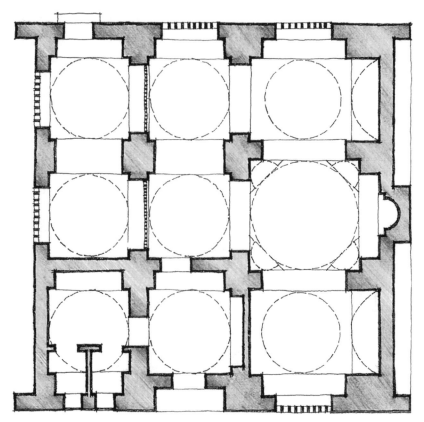

2.10: *Floor Plan, Dar al-Islam mosque, Abiquiu, New Mexico. Hassan Fathy, architect. Drawing prepared by Latif Abdulmalik after Hassan Fathy.*

ruvius's maxims, virtue, commodity, and delight. Fathy's architecture is anticlassical; his tectonic rules decide surface treatment and delineate spaces for rest, prayer, and contemplation. Fathy's reasoning consists of two orders:

1. The notion of created existence—a sense of space that is natural, esoteric, and human
2. The spirit of place, what Norber Schulz refers to as the genius loci, a spirit animated by reverence for the past and by a building tradition that mitigates the present

Fathy's plan for the New Mexico site is therefore a concept that appeals to the human spirit. Not only is there a tendency to consider the character of the site in terms of its psychological impulse, but it is, in a manner of speaking, a spiritual place: a container that is naturally contained. Fathy's concept of place, or *makan,* does not exist independently as a tangible form; it exists in the physical boundaries of human space. In other words, place and space are positive entities in which traditional categories of form and surface treatment can occur, but form and space are not ends in themselves. In this sense, Fathy's building tradition can be thought of as a leitmotif giving value and meaning to a sense of continuity. A building tradition is therefore a concordance and a synthesis of spatial qualities that are affordable, conventional, intelligent, and meditative. At Abiquiu, Fathy invokes building traditions from ancient Egypt as far back as the Nineteenth Dynasty, which he also used at the Gourna project in 1946. Fathy is fully aware of the ideological implications of these ancient building traditions, in the same sense that Palladio was aware of Vitruvius when he invoked his ordering principles. But there is a difference. Fathy's tectonic tradition is not a neutral or abstract expression; it is precisely meant to advocate and to reveal a structure of existence.

The Dar al-Islam example raises one more question: What are the elements that embody Fathy's architecture and/or express a quality of existence? Fathy's architecture influences human awareness of the universe and of people's coexistence with nature. No one can express the efficacy of this belief better than Fathy himself when he stated, "The best definition of culture is the outcome of the interaction between man and his environment in satisfying his needs both spiritual and physical. The physical is very simple. When we come to the spiritual, this is where the sensuality of man should recognize that something is beyond him."[40] This belief can be found in the Qur'an as well. In a sense, this statement argues for a balanced relationship with nature; it argues for a type of environmental equilibrium that isolates us from our mechanistic understanding of existence and puts us in a context in which we feel at home in the least amount of private space.

Fathy is not alone in his argument for morphological integrity and a quality of life that is environmentally sensible. E. F. Schumacher makes the same argument in his book *Small Is Beautiful,* as does Christopher Alexander in *A Pattern Language.* Ipso facto, Alexander endorses Fathy's beliefs, but Alexander defines the problem of building and dwelling in terms of a dichotomy between two types of existence, which he calls World-System A and World-System B. He defines system A as the ordinary way—a system of construction close to the site and the user, a system of common sense, a gradual process, much akin to the development of a fetus. System B is controlled by images and big money, and the building is seen as an object detached from human existence.

Fathy's Abiquiu scheme respects the natural topography of the site; it seeks a balance between organic and inert spaces and forms, as a sand dune responds to the wind. By responding in this way, he demonstrates a keen sensitivity towards human values and the natural and physical order of habitat: a totality of being.

We must understand the totality of being as simply the structure of existence; this structure is made relevant by Fathy's architectural vocabulary of traditional forms. His vocabulary gives his architecture human scale; it is this key constituent element in the tradition of tectonic space that is most fundamental. The vocabulary is animated by man-made elements: domes, vaults, porches, archways, and screens (or *mashrabiyyah*), just to mention a few.

Let us take for example the *mashrabiyyah;* it can be seen as a pattern of carved wood assembled through a particular geometry, or as a pattern of light diffused through a wooden screen. The simultaneous effect of matter and energy is expressed. Fathy's design of the New Mexico mosque employs a vocabulary of traditional ornamental motifs, which have been transmitted from one master craftsman or master builder to his apprentice. The final arrangement of these elements is a structure that produces an impressive spatial quality.

I have attempted to illustrate an overriding problem of aesthetic complexity apropos of the ordering of an American *masjid*. Owing to the importance attached by the community to the use of an extant aesthetic precedent, two idiosyncratic aspects of image, text, and form emerge: a collective memory imposes itself as an operative aesthetic device, along with a corresponding sense of historical continuity.

The American *masjid* is an edifice in evolution. In the very act of attempting to define its ordering principle, we are searching for a definition of a new but enduring regional identity—an identity with a sense of historical continuity. Art historians can contribute to the inquiry by aiding in a discourse that interprets the exigencies of meaning and the usage of an extant precedent. Allowing the embodiment of an intrinsic aesthetic meaning to become an objective component in the idiom and in the ordering of a new regional expression would help define more clearly the complexities of image, text, and form.[41]

More specifically and to the point: art historians, architects, and their Muslim clientele have much to share with one another in this discourse. An acute reading of the history of Muslim art and architecture can cultivate and direct the evolution of a set of aesthetic conditions for the American *masjid*.[42] Ultimately, these conditions would enhance the aesthetics of the American *masjid,* thereby allowing it to acquire an unconstrained regional character. The aesthetic disposition of the American *masjid* must recognize the element of historical continuity, but it must also exclude the use of aesthetic anomalies concerning the idiosyncrasies of image, text, and form.

A final question remains to be answered: How does one achieve visual affinity with an extant structure without hyperrationality or blatant mediocrity? From the examples presented above, the answer to this question remains an enigma. The enigma is even more apparent when the designer attempts to replicate rather than to interpret the features and structure of an extant building.

Furthermore, what happens when sentiment rules over architectural context? To conclude the discourse on image, text, and form, I would like to add another debate based on my reading of Hassan ibn Thabit and the observations of Abd al Qahir al-Jurjani, the eleventh-century Persian scholar of literary theory. In his memorial poem dedicated to the Prophet, Hassan ibn Thabit mentions several expressions that lament the loss of the Prophet and point to the emotional attachment to his mosque. In a specific mode, his use of language and syntax and his expressions evoke human desire and a sense of remembrance:

> In Madinah there are still traces of the Messenger, and a luminous abode of gathering—though traces may disappear and perish.
> The signs of a sacred house [*dar hurma*] are not effaced; in it the Guide's pulpit [*minbar*], which he used to ascend.
> Plain are the traces and lasting the landmarks; in his quarters [*rab*] a prayer place and a mosque.
> And the mosque which longs for his presence became desolate with only his *maqam* [station or place of standing] and *maq'ad* [place of sitting on the *minbar*] remaining as memorials.
> In it are enclosures [*hujurat*] wherein would descend God's light brilliant and bright.[43]

At first, both the *maqam* (station or place of standing) and the *mihrab* should be considered important. Since Ibn Thabit's expression is also a means of communication, his use of these words operates on two levels. The first is obvious, since the *mihrab* symbolizes the wall facing Makkah. The second meaning is attributed to the *maq'ad* (the place of sitting on the *minbar*); it conjures up memories of the Prophet and his immediate successors who used the same *minbar*. Therefore, these elements, which remain in use today in every mosque, are an articulate form of architectural communication. Abd al Qahir al-Jurjani presents us with two approaches to understanding language and syntax. The first is literal; it conceives language as mere words isolated from a context. The second conceives language as context only. These two approaches have their parallels in the aesthetics of the American mosque: one approach views fragments of aesthetic meaning as literal precedents handed down through history, independent of meaning or time; the other quotes the formal elements devoid of any meaning.

Al-Jurjani also suggests a way to construct accurate meaning. He argues that the significance of meaning must be harmonized and arranged in a way presupposed by the mind. This argument accepts sentiment and rationality. It is possible to decipher the aesthetics of the American mosque in similar terms. Hence, the existence of aesthetic elements and the associations they evoke no longer remain an enigma, since both are assimilated into the North American context. Assimilation changes the meaning of image, text, and form, as viewers understand familiar elements differently without necessarily recognizing what they mean altogether. In other words, reason and sentiment may be viewed as quests for meaning and ways to establish a sense of continuity. Therefore, architecture as a medium of aesthetic communication is an art of being and doing rather than seeing and showing. Undoubtedly, it also concerns the meaning and definition of truth.

We must ask one more question: Once an image is reproduced—because it can be so radically different from the original—does it capture the same essence as the original? The act of repetition may enact or facilitate a new idiom of expression, but this leaves the image wanting in terms of its true definition; this is a problem that many art historians and architects continue to face. Our study of the examples discussed in this chapter informs the discourse and continues the dialogue about the meaning of the past. I have attempted to frame a discourse on the aesthetics of the American mosque in the context of image, text, and form by looking at several examples of mosque architecture that embody meaning, aesthetics, and a rational composition of spatial components that define an architectural space for devotion. But rationality alone is not enough to decipher any problem of aesthetic treatment. Hence, the aesthetics of the American mosque reflect the sentiments of the American *ummah:* the mosque is both material and spiritual, inasmuch as image, text, and form demonstrate a cultural consciousness and a collective sense of belief.

SPACE, PLACE, AND
PUBLIC GATHERING

1. WHY SPACE MATTERS:
The Relevance of an Urban Mosque, Newark, New Jersey

Kevin Lynch, the renowned author of *Good City Form,* remarks that a "substantial equity of environmental access, at least up to some reasonable range of space and diversity of setting, must surely be one fundamental characteristic of a good city."[1] In general, Lynch's observation is correct; it is evident that the normative aspects of habitat in urban America maintain a spatial logic that is diverse, balanced, or mixed, with preference given to public space (i.e., space for public housing, shopping, working, schooling, worshipping, and recreating).[2] Our discussion of the urban mosque will suffice to explain a new type of urban institution that demonstrates a particular image of urban design, spatial diversity, and the use of public space. The congregational mosque, as one finds it in history, is the place of maximum collectivity and religious authority in a community; it is an academy of learning and the place where religious life falls into focus, where it gains social effectiveness and religious significance. In the medieval epoch, the congregational mosque was central to every town, village, or settlement, and since it drew to itself the largest crowds, it often had a central court open to the sky, to provide for overflow. Extant examples of this type of congregational mosque can be found in Fas (the Qarawiyyin Mosque), in Cordoba (the Umayyad Mosque of Cordoba), and in Isfahan (Masjid-i Jum'ah and Shah Abbas mosque, now known as Masjid-i Imam).

Recently attempts have been made to plan congregational spaces in urban America—although not on the same enormous scale as the three examples noted above—so that the urban mosque may retain a certain unity with the regional urban context and American environment. In part 5 of this chapter, I will introduce a theory of urban space for a New York mosque by an American Muslim architect, Professor Latif Khalid Abdulmalik. His theory must be discussed because it is an attempt to distinguish the various thematic modes of reading a space and, in a manner of speaking, two formative stages of design: embryonic and mature space.

In the urban milieu, the congregational mosque accepts certain types of nonreligious activities as well. Above all, it assumes a regional identity and an environmental image. There is a sound reason to discuss the urban mosque as a regional building type, since it has not received attention from Lynch in *Good City Form* or from others, and especially since it is a new civic nucleus and neighborhood center. Lynch has also argued that "a good environmental image gives its possessor an important sense of emotional security. . . . [I]t establishes a harmonious sense with the outside world."[3] Examples of what is meant by "environmental image" can be found in three regional urban mosques: (1) the mosque/office complex at Branford Place in Newark, New Jersey; (2) the Islamic Institute of Boston (IIB) in Roxbury, Massachusetts; and (3) the Muslim Center of Miami (MCM) in Miami, Florida. These three projects illustrate various ways public space "heightens the potential depth and intensity of human experience."[4]

Thus, the purpose of this chapter is to investigate the interaction between the design and the function of the urban mosque with respect to the aforementioned claims of religious distinction, that is, providing a public space for communal gathering and civic use. This type of inquiry has two objectives: (1) to demonstrate how and in what ways the urban mosque has influenced habitat in urban America (for example, how spatial and social alliances have evolved between the religious community and the public life around the mosque); and (2) to demonstrate how the urban mosque has integrated itself within the traditional urban context (thus far, the urban mosque does not appear to dominate the space of urban America as it did in a medieval Muslim city).

This inquiry can help us to clarify the issues raised by Lynch and others with regard to his concepts of image, public space, and the interaction between urban design and the environment. In this regard, we will attempt to identify what types of spatial nuances are different in the American context. It is not my intention to exaggerate the claims or the importance of the urban mosque. However, the urban mosque in America does promote various spatial attributes that have not been studied by urban historians, and so our discussion introduces a new debate and an objective inquiry concerning architecture and urbanism.

The first aspect of the debate concerns a legal account of the congregational mosque in medieval history. While the history of medieval Muslim cities provides an interesting background for a study of the urban mosque in America, a discussion about space and its relation to gender gives a more accurate account of the tensions that exist today with respect to the American environment. Part 4 of this chapter examines the lingering misconceptions about space and gender in order to explore some of the tensions between orthodox views and popular prejudices. Another aspect of the urban American mosque is its extended influence on the local community in terms of economic growth and social life. In what forms of political and religious exchange has the urban mosque principally affected the immediate community? Although the urban mosque may be characterized as a neoteric public space, intensely concerned with collective worship, its association with social, cultural, educational, and religious activities is equally important, since these activities serve the immediate community. The stability and presence of the mosque in urban America is therefore based on expectations informed by the practice of Islam.

A key aspect of the debate deals with spatial cognition related to the urban mosque. I am referring here to race relations and urban renewal. In what ways have both issues been affected by the presence of the urban mosque? The mosque at Branford Place in Newark, New Jersey, has been a positive catalyst in this regard. For instance, the gathering of various ethnic groups, ages, and sexes for daily worship and other pious activities takes place in the space of the urban mosque, and this collective awareness empowers the edifice with the primary role of a lawful public space. We are continuing to expand our account of the urban mosque.

The Branford Place mosque complex is an example that needs much more research, but I would like to raise at least a few points here that verify the arguments I have made above.

For a few decades, Branford Place was one of the forgotten streets of Newark. It was infested with drug and alcohol addicts; vagrant behavior was rampant. Today it is difficult to think of Newark without remembering the contrast of its urban past, which includes the spontaneous transformation of Branford Place. The presence of the mosque/office complex has reinforced the growth of commercial activities along the full extent of the street: *halal* (lawful) delis and restaurants, Muslim book stores, and stores that sell Islamic artifacts or cater to the needs of a Muslim and non-Muslim clientele. These types of business, as well as others located in the Muslim-owned building at 9 Branford Place, above the prayer halls themselves, have changed the identity of the area. The Muslim community worships daily in a provisional prayer space (*musallah*) on the second and fourth floors of the renovated office building, which was bought twenty years ago by a Muslim businessman. Because the Branford Place mosque/office complex is located in downtown Newark, the upper floors of the building are rented for a variety of uses: business offices, law offices, a Muslim school (one hundred students from pre-kindergarten to eighth grade, functioning from 1978–1998), medical offices, a computer school, social services, and a travel agency. These types of business activities help to demonstrate how the Branford Place mosque/office complex provides an aggregate of community services.

The greater Newark community contains a multinational congregation of twenty to thirty thousand Muslims.[5] The great majority of this number are African American Sunni Muslims, but the *musallah* at Branford Place is not restricted to or controlled by any single ethnic group.[6] On Fridays, the day of assembly (*yawm al-Jum'ah*), African American, Caribbean, Egyptian, Moroccan, Indian, Arab, Pakistani, and West African Muslim worshippers who reside in Newark and the surrounding areas frequent the congregation prayer, or *salat al-Jum'ah;* about seven hundred to one thousand men and women gather each week. Significantly larger numbers, ranging from three to five thousand, attend the *Eid* prayers (*Eid al-Fitr* and *Eid al-Adha,* which occur after Ramadan and Hajj) and the special *tarawih* night prayers during the fasting month of Ramadan. For over eight years, a unified *Eid* committee has held *Eid al-Fitr* and *Eid al-Adha* prayers in Westside Park at Twelfth Street and Eighteenth Avenue and in Weeqway Park.

Recognition of the urban mosque as satisfying part of the trend of urban revitalization in Newark has increased over time. Because the mosque/office complex is located in close proximity to Newark's city hall, city government officials are conscious of the major differences the presence of the mosque has fostered. City officials have made various concessions that satisfy part of the religious experience of the community. For example, the use of the mosque is sanctioned by city officials through exceptions they make to accommodate those who attend Friday worship: cars may be parked on

3.1: *Muslims performing the* **Eid** *Prayer, Newark, New Jersey. Photograph © 2000 by Amin F. Al-Khalil. Courtesy of Amin F. Al-Khalil.*

designated streets for an extended period of time during the Friday congregational prayer—roughly between one o'clock and two-thirty in the afternoon.

The Branford Place mosque/office complex has drawn attention to the commercial properties bordering the mosque, which in earlier times were abandoned buildings. The revival of commercial activity is one reassuring sign of a turning point in urban growth. The mosque/office building itself is interrelated to the rest of the urban fabric and to the public image of the Branford Place mosque over the past three decades. Public image and perception emphasize the importance of positive urban growth, considering that for the past three decades, since the mosque was established, the entire area surrounding the mosque has shown signs of urban improvement. The presence of the mosque/office complex has created a positive civic and religious node in downtown Newark; Muslims who work in the downtown area now have easy access to a place of worship.

In the early seventies, when a Muslim businessman first bought the Branford Place building from the city, the property surrounding the building showed signs of gross neglect. Many of the currently thriving storefront shops were boarded up or in run-down and dilapidated condition. The community immediately rallied around the mosque, sparking a renewal of attention to the social and economic integrity of the community. Today people congregate on Fridays on the sidewalk outside the mosque complex, where vendors sell their goods and the faithful engage in conversation or negotiate sales.

This atmosphere speaks of the pleasant sense of social relationship that the mosque has cultivated. Muslim-owned businesses sell fast food, household items, clothing, and religious books. Although it can be easily overlooked, the Branford place mosque has been a very positive urban influence: it has reduced the fear that comes with urban disorientation; it has contributed to a distinctive and legible character for the urban environment; and it has heightened the potential depth of the human experience. It has also enhanced the relationship between Muslim and non-Muslim residents, including the local government of Newark; it has created a positive relationship with members of the community at large. Although life in Newark is far from perfect, it may be argued that the mosque complex has improved the sense of well-being for Muslims and non-Muslims alike. The Newark mosque complex reveals how closely linked an urban mosque is to a sense of social and economic growth. It is more than a congregational space for worship; it plays a social role as well: space matters!

If the right of congregational worship, or the right to assemble, is guaranteed under the U.S. Constitution, then the existence of several places of gathering can be legally sanctioned in any locale in the United States. For example, Newark and the neighboring community of East Orange are served by a number of urban mosques: ashab al-Yameen, ahl al-Sunnah, Masjid Deenul-Lah, and others. Each mosque is no less significant than any other, inasmuch as they all serve the greater interest of the community. Each urban edifice has its own important node of religious and social activity, which helps to give distinction to the immediate neighborhood, and each also provides an obvious opportunity for change in the urban fabric of its neighborhood. Therefore, we can hypothesize that the urban mosque is a new urban American institution. It is a pious space that permits the tenor of life, work, education, and social and commercial activity to be tempered with a pause for prayer five times per day and with an opportunity for pious repose. A communal urban mosque is "sacred space"; it is capable of producing a positive social relationship with its physical setting. As with any good urban institution, the collective benefit that the mosque provides through the religious experience and its positive spin-offs cannot be overstated. According to police reports, in the neighborhood surrounding the ashab al-

Yameen mosque on Fourth Avenue in East Orange, New Jersey, the crime rate has dropped since the establishment of the community mosque ten years ago. In addition, commercial activities adjacent to the mosque have increased in the past five years.[7]

I mentioned above that quite frequently the congregations of the neighborhood mosques celebrate the *Eid* prayer together in public parks such as Weeqway Park or Westside Park. This is a good indication that the Newark community is indeed one community, since the members have agreed to make use of existing public space in various ways to fulfill the condition of congregational worship and social gathering (such as picnics) in an extramuros *musallah*.

The Branford Place mosque/office complex is a public space, but it has also served as a full-time educational organization that has provided much-needed Islamic instruction to young children and teenagers. For more than a decade, a highly trained and qualified resident *Shaykh* (religious scholar/preacher cum prayer leader), a native of West Africa, officiated at Branford Place. He was respected by the community for being a qualified scholar in Islamic law who could give legal opinions or interpretations of the law. He had a Ph.D. from New York University and earlier degrees in Islamic law (*shari'ah*) from the Islamic University of Madinah, Saudi Arabia. He provided needed guidance on legal questions and advice on marital issues and various aspects of worship. In addition, the mosque provides free access to women, who played active roles in the administration of the school, as well as in other community activities. Educational projects such as the Mosque Scholarship Committee, a committee run by youth and started by three African American Muslim women, regularly convene or hold events and fund-raisers at Branford Place.[8]

Only Jersey City rivals Newark in terms of religious activities and educational programs. Since the early seventies, Jersey City has had a vibrant Muslim community that worships at several urban mosques. Unlike Newark's Muslims, most of the Muslim residents of Jersey City are immigrants.

To some extent, the examples cited by Yvonne Yazbeck Haddad and Adair T. Lummis in their seminal work *Islamic Values in the United States* make it clear that every Muslim immigrant has had a long association with some aspect of Islam. The image these immigrants retain of the mosque is soaked in memories and meanings from the past. For example, Haddad and Lummis discuss how most immigrant communities view the role of the mosque in light of religious and social mores. They address various types of generational issues, which are sources of much discontent among Muslim immigrants, particularly Muslim women.

The Newark community is different in many ways, so it does not suffer from the identity crises or generational insecurities highlighted by Haddad and Lummis. Because the majority of Muslims in Newark are African Americans, the mosque is of special importance when we consider life in an urban environment. To aid in understanding its importance, I have highlighted how it has been perceived by the Muslim and non-Muslim communities. Each point in the general argument presented above indicates a sense of urban disposition linked to the primary activities of the mosque.

The social and religious needs of the Newark community, however loosely defined or understood, are important: after prayer, education is most essential, and the other types of social events that promote or enhance solidarity and group feelings must not be ignored. The Branford Place mosque complex has been successful in creating and maintaining a sense of community feeling analogous to medieval scholar Ibn Khaldun's term "asabiyyah," or group feeling.

We introduced the discussion of the urban mosque with Kevin Lynch's notion of good city form. City form is a human concept perceived in physical form. That is to say, the characteristics of habitat are both topological and psychological. The Branford Place mosque complex reveals the strength of both aspects of habitat.

It would be informative once more to restate a few general points of the foregoing discussion. One point of view treats habitat as a reflection of individual habits and collective behavior. It tries to isolate group feeling and religious conduct as a unique type of collective experience. For this reason, the concept of gathering requires that we identify human values and spatial principles, which are expressed in terms of space and place. A second point of view deals with the urban reality of space and place, which is also characterized by change; each change is fueled by a continuous search for an ideal mode of life in urban America that allows for full human participation and user satisfaction. The planning of a mosque in an urban environment offers additional ways to refine the relationship between the space of the edifice and the urban context. In the Boston neighborhood of Lower Roxbury, an attempt is being made to integrate a mosque and an educational facility (madrasah) into an existing urban context, and the scheme suggests a coherent synthesis of physical form and urban design.

2. THE IMAGE OF A PUBLIC SPACE:
The Islamic Institute of Boston, Roxbury, Massachusetts

There are unquestionably strong urban design tendencies that are identifiable by observing the cognition of the Muslim community and its sense of realism about life in urban America. Take for example the rational design and planning of a large architectural firm such as Steffian Bradley Associates (SBA), who have been commissioned by the Islamic Society of Boston (ISB) to design the Islamic Institute of Boston (IIB) for the Lower Roxbury neighborhood. The order and planning of the building are more or less controlled by the zoning regulations and the direction of the Boston Redevelopment Authority (BRA). The urban design approach offers a sequence of innovative relationships among all parties—the client, the BRA, and the architect. Such working relationships are unprecedented because they demonstrate a judicious application of building codes, land use, and open space in the context of an American urban tradition. The ISB project will be discussed below in further detail.

Because the interpretation of the term "tradition" is often vague, many incongruous types of images exist in urban America. These images are often visually hostile and spiritually vacant. While billboards and neon signs change, architecture is an enduring image that stays with us. Architecture and urban design pedagogy may assume the notion that an architectural image can be forged to give credence to urban fitness; some architects even believe the architectural image is a saving grace.[9]

Robert Venturi explains just how the quality of electrographics has disguised the shape and façade of buildings in a brief period of time.

> In Las Vegas, this evolution is compressed into years rather than decades, reflecting the quick tempo of our times: ugly and ordinary. However, since most of this ornament depicts structure—it is ornament symbolic of structure—it is less independent. The image of the structure and space reinforces rather than contradicts the substance of structure and space.[10]

In our time, image is a distortion of normality; it is ugly, ordinary, heterogeneous, popular, pastiche, and commercial, and it looks awful. With all our knowledge, reasoning, equivocation, and uncertainty about how we should build, what we should build, and how it alters the landscape, the debate remains with us. The term "image," which appears in Kevin Lynch's

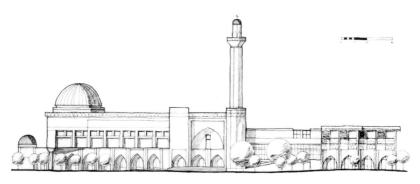

3.2: *Side elevation, Islamic Institute of Boston, Roxbury, Massachusetts. Steffian Bradley Associates Inc., architects. Drawing prepared by Paul Hanson after Steffian Bradley Associates Inc.*

The Image of the City, is mentioned with such frequency in order to explain the conditions that give rise to the possibilities of urban existence and urban intervention.[11] The source of Lynch's explanation is of course debatable, but it seems almost certain that his inquiry demands that we search again and again for the meaning and use of an image rather than for a litany of pre-scribed answers. A counterpoint introduces a contrast between two types of images: the visual order of urban America related to the use of the street or public setting, and the sensitive use of controlled image, which allows for the reinterpretation of a public space.

Deferring first to Lynch's theory of visual order and then to our own hy-pothesis of public space, we will discuss the proposed urban design for the Islamic Institute of Boston to demonstrate how an urban institute defines its own space and its own rules. In addition, we recognize how conventional building codes reinforce the sensitive functions of egress, scale, order, and control. Building codes are conventions that have been established over a long period of time in the city of Boston and throughout the United States. We will consider a few instances of how the application of the code affects public space and the development of the proposed urban design for IIB.

Three key questions form the basis of our inquiry: First, is there a re-lationship between image and code, between legal text and form? As an example, the translation of a legal code into an architectural image may result in an enhancement of architectural form rather than a limitation of space or function. Second, in what ways does the image abandon or inten-tionally express explicit forms of symbolism? As Robert Venturi points out,

"Sigfried Gideon called this artful contrast within the same building a gross contradiction—a nineteenth century split-feeling—because he saw architecture as technology and space, excluding the element of symbolic meaning."[12] Third, can the connections among public space, private interest, and spiritual intervention be interpreted as purely a religious adherence, which acknowledges divine existence? Because the mental universe of Islam has a well-established eschatological dogma, it presents unrestrained opportunities to obtain unlimited blessing (*barakah*) from God, without interchange of time or space. The believer perceives linear time in three appearances: in terms of revelation, in terms of physical space, and in terms of eschatology. For example, the *waqf*, or public endowment, sustains a relationship between life and death with regard to the blessings one receives without limitations of time and space. I will have more to say about this time-space relationship below.

These remarks are succinctly stated because it is my intention to expand the discussion using the IIB mosque/*madrasah* as an example. Consider the most visually symbolic image of the IIB mosque/*madrasah*, the minaret, which rises upward toward the sky. This vertical feature is reminiscent of an earlier historical epoch, a different place and time. Indeed, it recalls the first occasion when the call to prayer was made in Madinah in the year 622 C.E. by Bilal—the Abyssinian companion of the Prophet—from the elevated roof of the Prophet's mosque. Although the minaret is today highly symbolic, it retains positive value in which the architectural memory of the past is rooted. The very substance of the spiritual life of a community—what we may call religion, whether it is non-European (Asiatic, that is, Hinduism, Buddhism, or Islam) or Christian—is characterized by an objective inquiry to discover the mythic and symbolic aspects of primordial existence. Mircea Eliade demonstrates in numerous instances that primordial man, irrespective of his religious belief, reveals his deepest source of organic, natural, or primordial life. It is a life that is rich in myth, imagery, and symbolism.[13]

In Lower Roxbury, the 122.5-foot minaret will no doubt be a well-defined landmark and a symbolic image for the district; it will be an unforgettable sight. The minaret exceeds the 45-foot maximum height allowed in the community college subdistrict (where the mosque will be located) under the definition of building height in Article 2A of the building code. However, the code specifies that structures normally built above a roof that are not developed for human occupancy, such as domes, monuments, church spires and flag poles, are not subject to the maximum building height. As a result the forty-five-foot-height requirement is not applicable.[14]

If we pause for a while to consider Lynch's remarks, his thesis sustains an ongoing inquiry with regard to the theory and practice of architecture, urban design, planning, and public policy. In *Good City Form,* he explains how various modalities of urbanism tend to integrate the city or are essential to the value of urban life in the city. In light of my earlier remarks about image, code, and form, the integration of the IIB scheme into the urban fabric of the Lower Roxbury district is significant in two key aspects. First, the environmental image acts as a bearing; in terms of culture, it plays a symbolic role as well. It furnishes material for common memories and symbols, which serve as a vast mnemonic system for the retention of group history and ideals.[15] Thus, any observer or pedestrian can mentally identify the building's image in contrast to other types of commonly recognized spatial characteristics. Second, a signified environmental form may serve as a basis for the ordering of knowledge. For example, inasmuch as the minaret is located at the main entrance of the building at the intersection of Elmwood and New Dudley Streets, it can be used as an external reference when a person passes by or travels toward it from a distance.[16]

The urban design for the IIB scheme in the Lower Roxbury district achieves both of these aspects, but the scheme goes further; it embodies several positive architectural themes that promote social, religious, and cultural integration. First, the project is conscious of the differences it makes in this part of the city. It is programmed by the client, the Islamic Society of Boston, and the architect, Steffian Bradley Associates, to serve the social, religious, and educational needs of the immediate community. Second, the physical characteristics of the plan are thematic, consisting of a variety of architectural components: space, form, detail, symbol, building type, use, and activity. Third, it represents a striking opportunity for change in the urban landscape of Lower Roxbury. Its own inner program is congenially planned to be connected via a configuration of paths and physical references with surrounding elements, i.e., a public park, a community college, and a major recreation center.

Yet another design element reveals the inherent ordering of the site. The designers are forced to obey a primary ontological religious code, the orientation of the building towards Makkah, or the *qiblah* direction. But since

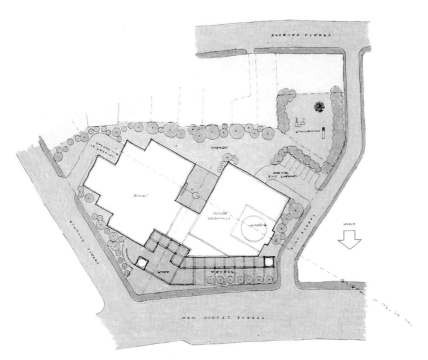

3.3 (a): *Site plan, Islamic Institute of Boston, Roxbury, Massachusetts. Steffian Bradley Associates Inc., architects. Drawing prepared by Paul Hanson after Steffian Bradley Associates Inc.*

we have discussed this form-making code and its concomitant symbol, the *mihrab,* in chapter 1, it will suffice to make only a few brief remarks here. Because identification of the Makkah direction of the *qiblah* must be made known to all worshippers, one may argue that the physical attributes of the site are immaterial, since the architectural configuration of the site plan is governed by this code.

The mosque/*madrasah* is planned according to an established axis of prayer that conforms with the obligation of facing Makkah (N60° 24′00″E). The building configuration and its orientation, therefore, are a conscious response to the Makkah orientation. The building layout has been arranged along another short axis pointing to the street intersection—the main pedestrian entrance—where the base of the minaret is located. The 69,950-plus-square-foot site is bounded by New Dudley Street on the north, Elmwood Street on the west, and King Street on the east. An entrance plaza serves as a transitional space between the urban streets and the community

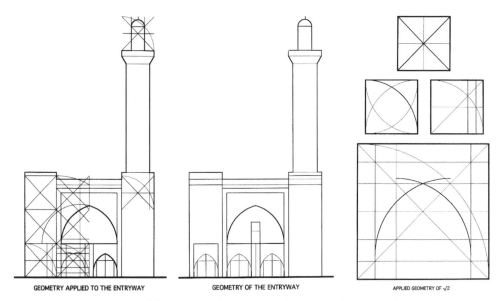

GEOMETRY APPLIED TO THE ENTRYWAY   GEOMETRY OF THE ENTRYWAY   APPLIED GEOMETRY OF √2

3.3 (b–d): *Geometry of the entryway, Islamic Institute of Boston, Roxbury, Massachusetts. Steffian Bradley Associates Inc., architects. Drawing/study © 2001 by Paul Hanson.*

center, and the plaza is surrounded with an open masonry arcade, plants, and benches.[17]

Conventional planning wisdom in our culture suggests that an educational facility should not only reflect but promote a desirable urban model to enhance social behavior, with the expectation and the understanding that it can produce and reproduce healthy social conditions. Existing smaller mosques in the greater Boston area (located at Quincy, Sharon, Intervale Street in Dorchester, Shawmut Avenue in Roxbury, and Cambridge) provide a limited aspect of these objectives. Likewise, prayer spaces are available to the Muslim student communities at Harvard, Boston, and Northeastern Universities and at Massachusetts Institute of Technology.

The plan of the IIB scheme includes: a mosque, 10,200 square feet; a community center, 26,200 square feet; a school (kindergarten to eighth grade), 26,000 square feet; and underground parking, 96 spaces.

The institute will help to fulfill the above mentioned expectations by putting emphasis on education and by making a positive gesture to its immediate neighbors, Roxbury Community College and James P. Timility Junior High School. The ISB has also indicated a strong interest in entering into an agreement with the city of Boston to support and contribute to the

Roxbury community by sharing in the provision of the following public amenities:

- landscape gardening and horticultural arts and sciences with Highland Park Community Gardens;
- family counseling and substance abuse counseling;
- an ongoing series of lectures on various aspects of Islam in connection with Roxbury Community College, and collaboration with the college on the development of a research library for Islamic law and the history of Islam;
- maintenance of play areas and a public park with the city of Boston; and
- coordination of a summer camp for the benefit of interested youth in the Roxbury community.[18]

Although the plan of the IIB is defined in terms of economics, one could argue that the scheme goes beyond its own economic considerations. Looked at exclusively from an urban design perspective, the scheme is designed to "respond to the architectural context of the Boston area."[19] The design objective of the project includes several regional features. It uses a contemporary Bostonian expression (with due respect for Islamic beliefs and architectural traditions) that closely relates to the urban context of its Roxbury neighborhood and is fully integrated with the existing site. The building's exterior is clad with reddish brown brick on a cast-stone base, with stucco relief to break up the massing of the façade. The stucco is used particularly at upper portions of the second floor to reduce the apparent overall scale of the building. These traditional New England materials commonly appear on buildings in Boston.[20]

Moving from the discussion of urban design to the aspect of public interest (*maslahah*), we find in an earlier period in Islamic history several similar examples of urban religious and educational complexes. These urban institutions provided free educational, medical, and social amenities for the public. Two examples are the mosque/*madrasah* of Sultan Hassan and the Qala'un complex, both in Cairo. Much larger examples include the Ottoman Kulliye at Edirne (built 1484–1488, during the reign of Sultan Beyazit II) and the Sulemaniye complex in Istanbul (built 1550–1557, during the reign of Sultan Suleman the Magnificent). When we consider these examples, we find a precedent for similar types of urban institutions today.

Traditionally, education nourished both the spiritual and the mental aspects of human nature. It endeavored to stimulate the soul and intellect by disseminating true knowledge. True knowledge consisted of revealed (intuitive) knowledge and acquired (deductive) knowledge. The former was known as the intelligence of the heart: inspired from the soul, poetic and imaginative by nature, and guided by faith.[21]

The IIB is intended to be a mosque/*madrasah* in this tradition; it will function as both a religious and an educational facility. The physical facilities, community center, mosque, and institute provide the individual and the society in Lower Roxbury with essential intellectual, religious, and social benefits. The significance of such benefits is an important ingredient in the institute's public value; furthermore, the handicapped, the poor, and subjugated races, classes, and genders will all have free access to the facility. One final remark remains to be made with regard to Lynch's *Good City Form* and M. Christine Boyer's chapter "The Inversion of Public and Private Space" from her book *The City of Collective Memory*. Lynch's reading of the city is generally a reasonable one; he recognizes the benefit of having mixed public and private spatial uses in a city. However, his theory of good city form is hardly commensurate with the concept of spiritual obligation, which occurs in the mosque via the daily reenactment of prayer. With regard to prayer, the roles of the church and the mosque are entirely different.

In Islamic practice, prayer is a personal encounter with the divine. In combining the community space with the religious space—through the communal performance of five daily prayers—the obligation of public interest and the religious obligation are combined. The merging of the public space with the space for the private devotional act takes on legitimate meaning; the emphasis is not only material but spiritual. The Qur'an sanctions this attitude; it repeatedly advises the faithful worshipper to support all acts of worship with private or public charity. One example of a private act that benefits the public in perpetuity is the individual *waqf*, or religious endowment.

This imaginative shift from private to public provides connections among the individual believer, public benevolence, and the recipient, the community. It is for this reason that we cite Boyer's idiom "inversion of public and private space." However, I use the idiom not exactly as she does but with a fresh interpretation, which subverts the definition of public space and private interest. The key aspect of the IIB scheme lays emphasis on our own thesis of private interest and public space; it recognizes the personal and religious obligation of all believers without ignoring the needs of the community. The design of the complex provides a convenient venue for sustaining this relationship. It is perhaps for this reason that many buildings were endowed for public use in medieval Cairo and elsewhere in the Muslim world; hence the *waqf* system brings together the physiological dimensions of space and time.

The foregoing discussion has been concerned with the setting out of a public space whose primary role is public benefit. The architect Abdel Wahed el-Wakil presents a radically different approach to the urban design problem we have discussed above. He understands architecture in terms of human existence and as an act of human creation that also maintains a relationship with the divine presence. Since there is never any attempt to represent the image of God or to define God in any form, shape, or fashion, Muslim art and architecture is aniconistic, but it is also sacred. El-Wakil's design proposal for a mosque and community center in Miami presents a spatial vocabulary that may be simply defined as a sacred space. We will now attempt a general interpretation of his design philosophy for the mosque and the community facilities that he designed for the Miami Muslim community.

3. THE PRODUCTION OF A SACRED SPACE:
The Muslim Center of Miami, Miami, Florida

As we have noted above, the American urban mosque is a public place that must respond to social and cultural as well as religious needs. In terms of its function as a public place, it favors worship as a key priority. In the building program for the Muslim Center of Miami (MCM), the client thoughtfully included the following types of activities as part of a program to meet the social, cultural, and religious needs of the Miami community: public lectures; communal gatherings for men, women, and children; day care; counseling; recreation; education; funerals; weddings; study; and prayer. In what way can these requirements be fulfilled, and what kind of architectural space would accommodate such a diverse set of activities? Furthermore, what kind of architectural identity could be forged to make the edifice appropriate to the Miami environment? These are key questions that affect the construction of Islamic centers throughout America. In brief, we are drawn

3.4: *Sulayman Palace, Jeddah, Saudi Arabia. Abdel Wahed el-Wakil, architect. Photograph* © *1983 by Akel Ismail Kahera.*

to one central question: How does one mix the secular with the sacred or the mundane with the spiritual? In the absence of proper design studies or building criteria for mosques in America, any design solution could easily become a contested space before it is built. There are no easy solutions or answers to these questions. Above all, any attempt to replicate an extant visual image from the Muslim world without fully understanding all design implications could be a fatal design error.

Because the mosque is a sacred building, many non–Muslim architects naïvely try to demonstrate to the client how a particular "Middle East" style of building may apply to the American context or to a given location. In proposing a naïve solution that is not well thought out, many architects try to replicate an extant visual image or building form. If the solution is guided by a well-established and tested language of architecture, a case could be made for the deliberate use of a style that fulfills the client's needs. Consider, therefore, the design for the Muslim Center of Miami, which was proposed by the internationally known architect Abdel Wahed el-Wakil. Many clients favor the particular style of building that El-Wakil has advocated since 1971, when he began his private practice. Since that time, El-Wakil has won much praise and many prestigious awards. He has designed over twenty mosques and several private residences in the Middle East; he has also prepared design proposals for projects in England and the United States. The Muslim Center of Miami is his first major work in the U.S.

The MCM is a non-profit organization that was established in 1978. The chief mission of the MCM is to establish a Muslim community dedicated to Islam in accordance with the true teachings of the Qur'an and the *sunnah* in the manner adopted by the Noble *Sahabah* (companions) and *As-Salaf as-Salih* (righteous predecessors).[22]

The five-acre site for the mosque and community center is located at the intersection of SW 72nd Street (Sunset Drive) and SW 123rd Avenue in Dade County, Miami, in a mostly residential area with residents of diverse

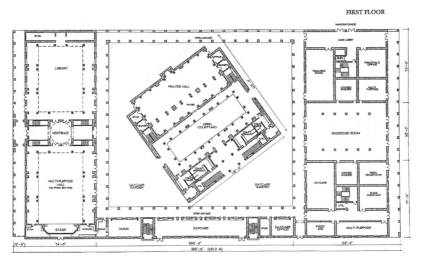

3.5 (a): *Site plan, Muslim Center of Miami, Miami, Florida. Abdel Wahed el-Wakil, architect. Reprinted by the permission of Abdel Wahed el-Wakil.*

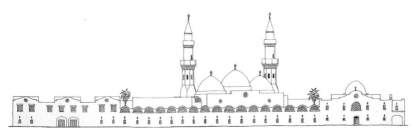

3.5 (b): *Elevation, Muslim Center of Miami, Miami, Florida. Abdel Wahed el-Wakil, architect. Reprinted by the permission of Abdel Wahed el-Wakil.*

incomes. For the estimated 30,000 to 110,000 Muslims who live in Miami, the site is accessible from Exit 20 on the Florida Turnpike, which connects major eastern Florida cities. The center will serve the needs of an ethnically diverse community that currently worships at three established locations and other smaller *musallah*s throughout the city. Three major educational institutions are located in close proximity to the MCM site: the University of Miami, Dade Community College, and Florida International University. The project brief states that the site was chosen to

> allow the center to be a living and visible monument for Muslims. Unlike more prominent locations such as downtown Miami where such a monument would stand tall in the day but dead and locked at night, this center may be used day and night by the business, residential and educational community and provide enough vitality to support its growth.[23]

In the above quotation, the community has clearly identified a common-sense argument that undoubtedly calls for the center and its mosque to be places of vivid activity. Since the basic issue is one of community, the first question for the design is whether this type of structure can reinforce an agreed-upon image for the community.

The complex is designed to provide the following social, educational, and religious amenities:

- a multi-purpose hall to be used for the school, gatherings, seminars, conferences, symposiums, and weekly Islamic programs;
- a library that will serve as a research center as well as an exhibit space and will also be available to non-Muslims (15,929 square feet);
- a day care/nursery for lower age groups;
- residential quarters for the school caretaker, the *imam,* and visiting scholars (11,104 square feet);
- an elementary and secondary school with twelve classrooms and four teachers' offices, computer and science labs on the second floor, and a gymnasium and offices for *daw'ah* (propagation) and the *imam* on the first floor (29,651 square feet);
- a kitchen and dining room to cater to the center's daily use and for special functions;
- the *masjid,* with prayer halls and toilet facilities (15,587 square feet);

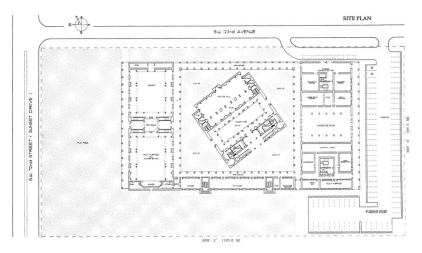

3.6: *Floor plan, Muslim Center of Miami, Miami, Florida. Abdel Wahed el-Wakil, architect. Reprinted by the permission of Abdel Wahed el-Wakil.*

- parking for eighty-two cars; and
- a generous playing field.[24]

The architect has placed these activities in two separate structures. The first structure is a rectangular envelope with a central courtyard, which is laid out on the cardinal grid of the site. The longer side of the rectangle (which runs north–south) is parallel to SW 123rd Avenue. The shorter side of the rectangle (which runs east–west) is parallel to SW 72nd Street (Sunset Drive). The second building is the mosque, an orthogonal structure with its own courtyard; it is located within the larger courtyard of the first structure.

The orthogonal plan of the mosque is rotated forty-five degrees to align with the *qiblah* axis. The domes and the minarets rise from the inner orthogonal structure. This juxtaposed arrangement is reminiscent of the layout of earlier structures. For example, the twelfth-century al-Aqmar mosque in Cairo retains alignment with the street façade of urban Cairo, while the inner space is oriented towards Makkah. Similarly, the Shah Abbas mosque of Isfahan, Iran, built during the reign of the Safavids, is connected to a large *maydan,* or public square, but is abruptly rotated to assume the Makkah axis. The rotation is not evident from the street façade in either case.

There are several layers of spatial treatment that are skillfully articulated, giving a particular character of uniqueness to the MCM facility:

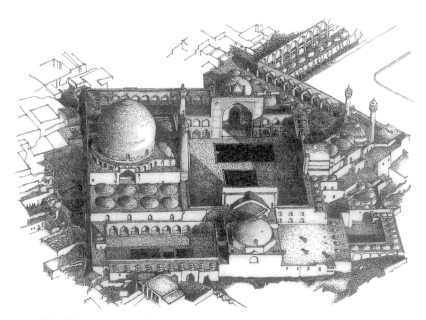

3.7: *Shah Abbas mosque (Masjid-i Imam), Isfahan, Iran. Drawing © 1994 by Latif Abdulmalik.*

- Space open to sky (the void: courtyard)
- Outer space (the solid building envelope: container)
- Inner space (the contained environment: center)
- Vertical space (the symbolic element: minaret)
- Spherical covering (the symbolic element: dome)

The combination of both types of enclosure, the container and the contained, reflects a rather innovative approach to the problem of orientation; this type of spatial treatment is really something quite different. The question, however, is not whether we should take the theory of inner and outer space literally but whether we can adequately explain the meaning of terms such as "inner space," "void," and "enclosure."

It is possible to answer this question, since there are obvious moments within the long history of Muslim architecture that point to the development of unique types of spaces that express inner space, void, or enclosure. We have already explained two examples of inner space, void, and enclosure, that is, the al-Aqmar mosque in Cairo and the Shah Abbas mosque in Isfahan (now Masjid-i Imam). Both examples demonstrate how built form responds to a particular concept of spatial orientation. For instance, it is no coincidence that the vast oblong—which measures 1,709 feet by 525 feet— adjoining the Shah Abbas mosque is called *naqsh-e-jahan* (image [=center] of the world). In this case, the Shah Abbas mosque connects the mundane environment to a sacred space. Perhaps the concept of center has a double meaning: In the first sense, it brings the landscape close to men and women. In the second sense, it carries an ontological meaning; it orients men and women toward a universal symbolic center (for example, the Ka'bah at Makkah), and thus the term "landscape" relates to the world in general.

Keeping this concept in mind, we may also argue that the act of building is analogous to the structure of emotions felt by each individual, since it explains how we understand symbolism and in what way symbolism embodies temporal and spiritual meaning. The architectural elements—courtyard, dome, minaret, container, solid, and void—give the concept of sacred space a temporal as well as a spiritual interpretation.

In one sense, we may define the entire space of the mosque as a wall facing Makkah with or without a spherical covering. But the physical conditions of this type of space demand human participation, such as the call to prayer or a gathering of worshippers who are regularly engaged in the act

3.8: *Interior detail, Muslim Center of Miami, Miami, Florida. Abdel Wahed el-Wakil, architect. Reprinted by the permission of Abdel Wahed el-Wakil.*

3.9 and 3.10: *Interior detail, Muslim Center of Miami, Miami, Florida. Abdel Wahed el-Wakil, architect. Reprinted by the permission of Abdel Wahed el-Wakil.*

of prostration. These communal acts give the space a common identity and above all a connection with the divine; hence, the character or sacredness is completed.

El-Wakil explains the concept of sacred space as a religious ideology. The sources of the ideology are the Qur'an and the *sunnah;* architectural methodology is therefore not a personal thesis.[25] The final part of this discussion will reflect specifically upon El-Wakil's theory of sacred architecture in relation to design of the Muslim Center of Miami. My first encounter with El-Wakil's work was in the early eighties, while I was working as a professional architect and living in Jeddah, Saudi Arabia. Daily I would observe master masons and craftsmen at work on the Sulayman Palace not too far from my office, and later I witnessed three of his Jeddah corniche mosques under construction. His list of completed projects in Saudi Arabia now includes the King Saud mosque, Jeddah; the Qiblatain and Kuba mosques, Madinah; and many other notable buildings. El-Wakil is not merely a didactic architect; he understands his trade with admirable passion because he was taught by an esteemed master, Hassan Fathy. The inspiration of the master remains with the student in his mind, in his heart, in his soul, in his speech; it comes out in his architectural expression, especially in houses of prayer.

Each time I enter one of the mosques El-Wakil has designed, it is a spiritual encounter. These highly articulated spaces provide a soothing feeling, truly pertinent to a place of spiritual repose. I never feel the urgency to leave the mosque, because the sensation is spiritually uplifting. Although individual spiritual experience cannot be adequately explained, this humble description conveys my own definition of sacred space.

El-Wakil himself is a master of expression; his architecture is pure, genuine, calm, distinct, and imaginative. He argues that "architecture is a collective duty, not an individual art, and it has its own vocabulary, that communicates the image in a meaningful way. . . . Every word in the vocabulary of the craftsman is related to form."[26] Traditionally, craftsman and architect/master builder share a similar vocabulary, so the architect is not free to invent autonomous forms. The following remarks, which were made by Hassan Fathy, emphasize the relationship between craftsman and architect, but they also emphasize the canons of sacred art.

> The architect has to remember that wisdom does not belong to a unique epoch, it belongs to all times. It is present today as it was yesterday, and can be realized by anyone who desires it and who deserves it. Nowadays the procedure and methods of design and building have changed from

3.11: *Corniche mosque, Jeddah, Saudi Arabia. Abdel Wahed el-Wakil, architect. Photograph © 1985 by Akel Ismail Kahera.*

Sufi master craftsman to the architect-contractor system in which design and execution of the work are split, and the canons of sacred art are lost.[27]

Fathy's remarks are meaningful because Muslim architecture represents a nexus of temporality; hence, knowledge of being shares a meaningful relationship with idioms of architectural expression. Perhaps the statement that is farthest from this concept is Descartes's "*cogito ergo sum*" (I think therefore I am). Descartes's declaration illustrates precisely the split that Fathy mentions. *Cogito ergo sum* suggests that thinking and awareness of thought are the real substance of being, but it also celebrates the separation of the mind from the body and other activities of being. This Cartesian maxim, which has been adopted in the West to describe reality, is related to the crisis of architecture, which is of course also a human crisis. In Islam, man is not the center of the universe (*homo universale*); neither is he the measure of all things (*pan-ton met-ron an-thro-pos* = πάντων μέτρον ἄνθρωπος). The Cartesian split widened with the rise of historicism when a major rupture occurred between two formerly inseparable parts of the same profession: the craftsman and the architect. The responsibility for the entire imaginative realm of building was given to the architect, with diminishing recognition of the craftsman. Conscious of the split, El-Wakil explains his work as an act of devotion, and he observes that in the past, the mosque was one example of an ideal spiritual abode.

> Work is prayer. It is an act of devotion. . . . [Y]ou cannot dissociate work from belief. If you take Islam as a way of life, of which Islamic architecture is a part, a man's work is his mission on earth.[28]

In Islamic art and architecture, this aspect of human existence and other elements of human creation are direct manifestations of humans' understanding of the divine presence, which is known as *tashbih*. However, in Islamic art and architecture, there is no attempt to represent or define God. To return to the architect's involvement in the design process, certainly the range of meanings for "spiritual" is linked to a cosmology that does not eliminate the ultimate effect of traditional building techniques whose tectonic secrets were controlled by the craftsman. Both Fathy and El-Wakil added to their own cores of knowledge by working with master masons and by setting down exemplars derived from the experience of the master masons. El-Wakil's architecture embodies two primary aspects that appeal to the human spirit. First, the character of his mosques, in terms of its psychological effect, is, in a manner of speaking, both container and contained. Second, the container does not really exist independently as a tangible form, but rather, it exists in the consciousness of the beholder, who visually perceives physical boundaries of space while the intellect perceives the spirit of those elements that are contained.

Thus, El-Wakil would argue that postmodern architecture is self-indulgent because it seduces the architect and users alike by making them neglect the real essence of beauty, thus concealing the purpose of being. The failure of postmodern architecture can be attributed to the fact that it is disembodied from belief in the divine, and it is for this reason that our secular understanding of beauty has interfered with our concept of existence, or vice versa. Not so long ago, John Ruskin wrote in *The Seven Lamps of Architecture* about sacrifice, truth, power, beauty, life, memory, and obedience. These seven appearances exist in the sacred architecture of Islam.

The effect that each appearance has on the human mind is related to both remembrance and repetition. Just as the *mu'adhdhin* repeats his intonation five times daily to call the worshippers to prayer, so too does the mosque empower the faithful to orient themselves in space and time to the Ka'bah. Herbert A. Simon explains this relation to the environment as largely a reflection of human behavior and cognition.

> A thinking human being is an adaptive system; his/her goals define the interface between the inner and the outer environments. To the extent that he/she is effectively adaptive, his/her behavior will reflect characteristics largely of the outer environments (in light of his/her goals) and will reveal only a few limiting properties of his/her inner environment—of the physiological machinery that enables him/her to think.[29]

What do these remarks tell us about human thinking and cognition? First, they tell us that in large part, "human goal-directed behavior simply reflects the shape of the environment in which it takes place."[30] Second, they tell us that the full implications of daily worship and the space of assembly have not been drawn by psychologists.

From its practice in daily life, we could say that there is something intelligible about the harmony of perfection and repetition; religious practice is a form of perfection. This is perhaps what John Cage tried to express when he spoke of a liberating effect in his musical compositions, but failing to understand the essential quality of being, he decided on a fragmentary composition devoid of spirit and perfection. Because El-Wakil understands the quality of spirit and perfection well enough to avoid the conflict of fragmentation, his architecture engages various aesthetic codes in order to retain a sense of sacred engagement; that engagement effectively liberates the human spirit.

4. TIME, SPACE, AND GENDER:
The Place Where the She-Camel Knelt

I have by no means exhausted the list of examples I could cite to explain or support my hypothesis concerning the characteristics of an American mosque. I undertake a fresh discussion here, which is devoted to the topic of time, space, and gender. It will address the implications of how public space is organized and how legal interpretations affect the division of space in an American mosque. It could be argued that in many instances the division of space is biased against women and is therefore illegitimate from the viewpoint of the *shari'ah*. Historically, the debate is fairly well documented. In 1911, at a conference held in Egypt, a complaint was made about the legal rights of women who had been denied the right to perform public worship and to enter the mosque. The woman who led this campaign was Bahithat al-Badiyyah. She based her argument on the fact that the Prophet had said, "Don't prohibit the female servants of Allah from entering the mosque," because she realized that women's right of public worship had been neglected by both women and men due to religious ignorance.[31]

Almost ten decades later, the debate still exists. It would seem that Bahithat's complaints apply to women in the U.S. as well, since women are sometimes characterized as moving between and within the spatial domains controlled by men. So it seems that there is an understood hierarchy between the possible use of public space and the perception of gender, which is influenced by particular regional customs or habit. Take for example a proclamation issued in 1955 by a zealous governor that made the congregational prayer compulsory for women at an earlier time of the day, separate from men's prayer. The *mufti* (jurist) of al-Azhar, Mahmoud Shaltout, issued

3.12: *Ladies' entrance, Sligh Street Mosque, Tampa, Florida. Photograph © 1999 by Asad Siddiqui. Courtesy of Asad Siddiqui.*

a convincing *fatwa* (religious legal opinion) against the ridiculous decree. Shaltout's *fatwa* reads as follows:

> There is no special *jum'ah* [Friday congregational worship] for Muslim women and no differentiation in time and place in this prayer between male and female. The consensus of opinion of all the Muslims past and present is that there should be no special prayer for women. But they can pray—if they wish to attend the *jum'ah*—with men in one *jamaat* [congregation] behind the same *imam* with the same *khutbah* [sermon] in the same place, but they should line up behind the men. This is something common to the five daily prayers, the two *eid* prayers and the pilgrimage. It is one of the distinguishing features of Islam to unify the Muslim community in its general worship and abolish all individual distinctions regarding standing positions of piety and sincerity to God, the Knower of what is secret and what is apparent.[32]

The remarks in Mahmoud Shaltout's *fatwa* are sensitive to the rights of women, but they are also intimately associated with the public domain. His *fatwa* overrules all restrictions that have been put on women and limitations that have been placed on public space. Dr. Taha Alalwani, a prominent Muslim who teaches a course on *fiqh* (Islamic jurisprudence) of Muslim minorities at the Graduate School of Social Sciences in Leesburg, Virginia, argues in favor of an application of the *shari'ah* that is responsive to a pluralistic, multicultural, and multiethnic environment. "The centrality of the environment in *fiqh* is not new and is in line with the counsel of scholars of the past who paid attention to the person asking the question and the conditions of habitat."[33] Alalwani's explanation of the nuances of *fiqh* and environment is demonstrated further in the following remarks.

> Imam Shafi'i [d. 204/820] developed his school in Baghdad, where he wrote his famous treatise in *fiqh* and *usul*. However upon leaving Baghdad and settling in Egypt he altered his opinion on all but 13 issues, on account of the changed environment and situation.
>
> We need a lot of understanding from our *Fuqaha* and *Ulema* [jurists] in the North American environment, and if they issue *fatawa* without studying this environment, they will be doing a great disservice to the North American community. Indeed their rulings or rather their

misinterpretations will have a serious effect on the future of Islam on this continent.[34]

Public behavior affected by habitat might subsequently be understood better if we use the mosque as a social index, because it is a public gathering space for men and women.

While the mosque remains a public space, it has become decreasingly pluralistic, and alternative types of spaces tend to exclude women from appearing in the public domain or participating in the right of public worship. Within the scope of this discussion, we can merely raise a number of relevant questions and outline a few problems related to space and gender; further in-depth research is needed to address these issues. In recognition of the importance of social mannerisms, specifically the way spatial patterns implicitly affect behavior, our inquiry will examine the function of the congregational mosque—a public gathering space—as it relates to tensions connected to religious practice.

Since the death of the Prophet, the congregational mosque has become a legally "contested space."[35] The seminal edifice was attached to nine inner apartments; these domestic rooms were later destroyed by the succeeding caliphs to expand the building.

Since the Qur'an is silent on a specific spatial formula for a *masjid*, it is the *hadith* that provides a description of the site where the she-camel knelt. Ayesha, the wife of the Prophet, related that

Allah's Apostle stayed with Bani 'Amr bin 'Auf for ten nights and established the mosque [mosque of Kuba] which was founded on piety. Allah's Apostle prayed in it and then mounted his she-camel and proceeded on, accompanied by the people till his she-camel knelt down at [the place of] the Mosque of Allah's Apostle at Madinah. Some Muslims used to pray there in those days, and that place was a yard for drying dates belonging to Suhail and Sahl, the orphan boys who were under the guardianship of 'Asad bin Zurara. When his she-camel knelt down, Allah's Apostle said, "This place, Allah willing, will be our abiding place."[36]

After the *hijrah* (migration) to Madinah from Makkah in the year 622 C.E., the Prophet Muhammad faced the decision of choosing a place to abide. He did not want to show a preference or privilege to anyone by accepting an offer from among the people of Madinah. He decided to build his house and mosque at the place where his she-camel stopped. Initially there were two apartments, but later these were increased to nine for the Prophet and his wives. Each apartment was given to one of his wives, and the rest of the mosque was dedicated to communal use. The apartments were labeled *hujurat, buyut,* or *manazil* (domestic rooms, dwelling spaces). When the Prophet constructed Ayesha's apartment, he opened a door in the wall of the mosque that faced Ayesha's apartment. The mosque and her room were so close that the Prophet had only to lean his head from the mosque to Ayesha's doorstep.

The expansion of the seminal structure altered the configuration of the *masjid.* Al-Samhudi's *Wafa al-Wafa* describes in great detail the major alterations that took place on the seminal building; it appears that no designated space was set aside for women in the new configuration. This would suggest that the allowances that were made for women to use the building during the lifetime of the Prophet were restricted in later periods.

As far as the question of space and gender is concerned, the house and mosque of the Prophet serves as an example for the Muslim community, just like the other key components of his *sunnah.*

In reviewing the historical situation, we can understand why contemporary conditions of space and gender remain a subject of much controversy.

Cultural conventions, such as the importance of granting women free access to the mosque, persist as a result of impractical legal interpretations. The nuances of space and gender are also products of time, which becomes visible through religious practice; thus, "time clashes with time."[37] In the contemporary urban milieu, these clashes continue to occur; hence, conflicts of time and space are no less significant than they were in the twelfth century C.E. Our upcoming discussion of a legal debate from twelfth-century Muslim Spain will demonstrate interpretations of public gathering.

Through the widespread appearance of custom and the congregational requirement, the urban milieu of the Muslim community in America demonstrates nuances of time, space, and gender and the efficacy of the urban mosque. Above all, the urban mosque is a place where religious experiences are shared or transformed. It is also a place where patterns of religious conduct are fully differentiated or self-consciously expressed.

If we examine the patterns of spatial use and behavior among immigrant Muslims and indigenous Muslims, documented incongruities in the aforementioned patterns of cultural conduct illustrate nuances of public gathering. On one side, we find the self-conscious individuality of the Muslim immigrant group with an extant repository of cultural values and religious norms.

On the other side, we find an indigenous community, which holds within its own social and cultural framework reverent attitudes that are expressed in an entirely different manner.

Public gathering maintains the religious shape of the first group, and it externalizes collective forms of identity for the second. In both instances, the urban mosque is a communal entity that symbolizes the collective practice of Islam.

Orthodoxy means different things to different people, but among indigenous Muslims, the meaning is even further complicated with regard to religious practice. Because an underdeveloped interpretation of Islamic law exists within the indigenous community, religious practice manifests itself in many different forms. First, no particular school of thought (*madhhab*) holds sway over another. This can be an advantage, but it is also the source of much dispute. Second, diaspora scholars (scholars from the Muslim world) who advocate a preferred legal opinion based on a particular country of origin or *madhhab* offer textbook responses to unprecedented issues. Third, African American scholars from within the indigenous community are few; their legal influence is not widespread, especially within the immigrant community; and for the most part, they are not trained to exercise *ijtihad* (independent reasoning). Finally, a general lack of scholarship exists among the *imams* and *khatibs* who run local *masajid*. At the moment, there are problems with consensus (*ijma*), in which case the opinion of a local *imam* is often controversial. If we take the issue of public space, gender is currently the main subject of the discussion.

One explanation for this controversy has to do with distinction in dress, which the Qur'an advises for women. Women are required to wear the *hijab* (veil) in the public domain; the public domain can be defined as anywhere a woman shares the public or domestic space with a male counterpart who is not related to her by marriage or blood. Women are regarded as the center of the argument because the separation of male and female space has gradually resulted in the total seclusion of women from public space and in some instances has restricted their access to the mosque. In America, environmental circumstances and the pressure of urban life affect opportunities for social interaction. The urban mosque gives rise to alternative modes of use and new channels for renewed social interaction.

Take for example the following remarks, which were made by a female Muslim immigrant:

> Women who are living in a non-Muslim country [America] want to feel like they belong to a Muslim community and the only way to get this feeling is by going to the mosque. One Egyptian Muslim said that the only time she has contact with other Muslims is when she gets together with her friends or when she goes to the mosque. There are no other Muslims where she works or in her neighborhood. As a working mother, it is hard for her to find time during the week to meet her friends. Her weekend trips to the mosque are the only time when she can meet new Muslims and feel like she is part of a group or community.[38]

Since the congregational mosque retains a commonly understood historical function, it is fundamentally similar to the Prophet's mosque; as far as men and women are concerned, both have free access to the mosque to exercise the right of social gathering and religious practice. The right of communal gathering is a critical aspect of religious practice; it has been a debate among Muslim jurists in the past, and it remains a contested issue today. In the medieval Muslim world, the public domain of a town, country, village, or city admitted the development of a legal discourse that was cognizant of the use of public space with regard to age, sex, and gender but gave preference to men. This will come as a surprise: many contemporary Muslim jurists share the same medieval views. Therefore, they have not thought about the public domain with respect to the American community, or in an analytical manner with respect to time, place, and the conditions of life in urban America. It is for this reason that controversy prevails between a distorted, medieval view that women should pray at home and a judicious view that women should have equal access to the public domain.

The debate brings to light certain historic problems of interpretation with regard to gender and the long-term controversy about public space. It is for this reason that we discuss the long-standing debate in this chapter. First, we will revisit the controversy concerning the legal right of women to congregate and the implications of legal opinions (*fatawa*) concerning public worship and public gathering. Second, we will consider various extant interpretations of the Qur'an and the *sunnah* in order to shed light on the debate.

Historically, the urban habitat of the Islamic city is endowed with a sense of spatial equity. For example, a correlation exists between the performance of congregational Friday prayer (*salat al-Jum'ah*) and the location, size, and placement of a mosque within every Muslim city. Habitat disputes about the use or orientation of a mosque or a *musallah* (a provisional space set aside for congregational worship) are not uncommon among Muslims in urban or rural America. The interpretation of the *qiblah* direction is one key debate, which was taken up by two scholars from Philadelphia. Al-Hajj Riad Nachef and Ashaykh Samir al-Kadi, both of the Ash'ariyyah creed and the Shafi'i school, published a treatise entitled *The Substantiation of the People of Truth That the Direction of al-Qibla in the United States and Canada Is to the Southeast.* The treatise is intended to resolve the precise direction of the *qiblah*, which should be taken into account—when building a mosque or in standing for prayer—to avoid the occurrence of a religious infraction. Nachef and Al-Kadi hold the opinion that the *qiblah* direction is to the southeast from North America, which differs from the commonly held practice of facing the northeast (using the great circle). To support their contention, Nachef and Al-Kadi present a thorough explanation based on Qur'anic exegesis and the opinions of several jurists, as well as calculations from geographic societies, universities, marine institutions, and astronomers. Similar disputes existed among medieval jurists concerning the status of a congregational mosque. Take for example the following case:

> In the medieval settlement [*rabad*] of Basta [in southern Spain] the Muslim community discussed the conditions that legally allow two congregational mosques in the same locale to have Friday prayers at the same time.[39]

One group of Muslims, group A, noted that no legal conditions would allow two concurrent congregational prayers in a village, town, or city, especially in a new mosque—a mosque that had been recently expanded. Therefore, group A decided to pray in the older mosque. Another group of Muslims, group B, argued that there were indeed some conditions that allowed for having the prayer in the newly expanded mosque, the larger of the two. Unable to resolve the dispute, they put the question to three different *mufti*s, asking them if it is allowed to have two concurrent congregational prayers in the same locale.[40] The *mufti*s differed in their legal rulings (*fatawa*), but two of them agreed on various aspects of the case, based on similar cases that had been discussed by earlier jurists.

First *fatwa:* Basta is a rural settlement; the residents are few in number, and they live outside the ramparts of the city (*ahl al-rabad*); therefore, they should perform the prayer at only one mosque. The *mufti* stated that because the mosques (new mosque and old mosque) were only 145 paces apart, the residents faced no great obstacle or hardship that would justify having two places of worship.[41]

Second *fatwa:* A generous number of worshippers would make a case for congregational prayers in the larger and newer of the two mosques. Thus, it may be valid given the conditions of necessity (*darurah*), which are as follows: (1) if, when people pray, they cannot follow the *imam* because the mosque is too crowded and they have to pray far from the mosque, it is allowed to have two *jum'ah* prayers in the same city; (2) if the town has two constituent parts and between them there is a river, it is allowed to have the congregational prayer on each side of the river (as, for example, in the city of Fas). The Maliki scholars agree to allow two *jum'ah* prayers in the same city where there is such a legal necessity (*darurah*). In al-Andalus, the scholars allowed two mosques and two concurrent congregational prayers; it became the *amal* (legal practice). Therefore, it is preferable to follow this *amal* because disagreement among people is harmful.[42]

Third *fatwa:* According to the scholars of the Maliki *madhhab,* there are three opinions: (1) the congregational prayer should only be performed in one mosque, according to Malik (d. 179/795) and Shafi'i (d. 204/820); (2) it could be done in more than one mosque in a big city, if there is a necessity (*darurah*); and (3) when the city has two or more parts and in between them there is a river, which creates a hardship, it is allowed to have more than one *jum'ah* prayer.[43] This *mufti* concluded that it was preferable not to prevent the prayer in the newer and larger mosque because it had been in use for thirty years, and during that time many scholars had accepted it (there was *ijma,* or consensus, among them). To oppose that practice would cause confusion and disturbance. He cautioned the Muslims, "*Sakinu wa la tunafiru*" (Be tranquil and repose; don't become ruffled, and don't create antipathy, repulsion, alienation, and estrangement).[44]

I cite the case of Basta for two reasons. First, although the idea of community life in the settlement of Basta has evolved since that time period, contemporary Muslim jurists continue to think of the urban mosque in the same light. They have not contextualized the case in a realistic manner or in the interest of the contemporary community. Second, consideration of the arguments in the Basta case is fundamental to our discussion of public gathering and the role of public access to space because it links the interpretation of legal opinion to the right of public gathering.[45] The legal discussions are consistent with the "pray at home" view that has been imposed on women, in light of the fact that the arguments proclaim everything possible while remaining silent on the issue of women. However, the three *fatawa* use legal terms, which speak of the immanent need to discuss the actual configuration of space. Many parallels can be found in the U.S., illustrating unresolved aspects of the discourse. It is for this reason that ambiguities remain, and they add to the notorious confusion about the use of public space. Thus, gender bias has become increasingly visible even in the non-Muslim world.

The performance of congregational prayer in Islam can be perceived as a defining condition of religious practice from two aspects. First, congregational Friday prayer is an important legal, public duty; however, its obligation is conditional. The congregation is calculated on the basis of the total adult male population or the aggregate permanent family units that exist in a town, city, or village. This legal injunction exists because Muslim jurists have not reached a consensus as to how many adult male individuals constitute a congregation (*jama'a*); the range of numbers that have been proposed includes three, five, seven, twelve, twenty, and forty.

Ibn Siraj (d. 750/1349), a well-known Maliki jurist of the city of Granada, was asked about the number of people (male worshippers) who have the right to establish congregational prayer (*jum'ah*) in a village. Apparently, the villagers had already instituted the *jum'ah* prayer with eight, ten, or twenty men in attendance. He ruled that a group of eight, ten, or twenty does not constitute a congregation. Furthermore, he insisted that the Maliki scholars had set the number at thirty to fifty men; therefore, if there are fewer than thirty houses in a village, the *jum'ah* is not valid. Ibn Siraj completed his *fatwa* with the remark that a large group of (male) worshippers, i.e., thirty or more, is highly valued in order for the community to observe the pride of Islam.[46] Hence, the inhabitants of a village, city, or town that has met the legal quota of adult male residents or permanent households are under legal obligation and are required, ipso facto, to perform the congregational prayer.

The congregation rule remains legally binding for those Muslims who follow the Maliki school of law, although other jurists of the same school have agreed that twelve people would constitute a congregation. Innumerable differing legal opinions concerning the congregation rule are observed by communities in Muslim and non-Muslim areas of the world today. In the American environment, the congregational rule, which limits the number of male worshippers, does not apply, since the basis and the conditions on which it was originally instituted were governed by a particular type of habitat. That type of habitat, that is, contiguous dwellings whose occupants are adherents of the faith and are all male heads of households, does not exist in urban or rural America.

The spiritual homogeneity of the American community is symbolically meaningful; therefore, the community sanctions the mosque as the key public space without consideration for the remarks made by Ibn Siraj or other medieval jurists. If we follow Ibn Siraj's argument, legal rationality recognizes the physical homogeneity of any Muslim community.

As far as the American community is concerned, the physical conditions do not exist; therefore, the legal definition of the term "congregation" (*jama'a*) now includes women and children—and even non-Muslim guests—which makes it inconsistent with the medieval interpretation mentioned above.

One way to clarify the meaning of the term "*jama'a*" and to demonstrate how it may not directly apply to American Muslim communities is to study the gender implications of its use. If we examine the most irrational and abstract use of the term "*jama'a*," we find that the widespread tenacity for telling women that they should pray at home and not in the mosque does not find consensus in the West. When we consider the time-space relationship of this particular congregation law to urban America, we face a more complicated picture.

Our environment is still a fundamental part of the experience of American life. The smallest space that is set aside for congregational worship in any American town, city, or neighborhood mosque is always cognizant of the women's attendance and participation in the communal prayer. Hence, it is not possible to apply the medieval congregational rule that uses the number of male worshippers as the only criterion without displaying inequality between the sexes. Here is one area, that is, the use of space, that the proper application of the *shari'ah* would defend—especially on the basis of necessity (*darurah*)—since equal access to the mosque by any individual, male or female, is a religious duty and therefore a legal right.

In America, Muslim women frequent the mosque with the same regularity as men and therefore cannot be excluded from the literal or practical meaning of the term "*jama'a*," or public gathering.

If our observations are accurate, a new debate about space and gender emerges as we study the American mosque; it places emphasis on the right of public gathering vis-à-vis the conditions of habitat. Hence, the definitions of spatial plurality, gender, public domain, and congregation have been taken into consideration in our discussion. Without laying claim to a completely new form of urbanism, our hypothesis concerning habitat and the right of public gathering assigns importance to the public space of the urban mosque. Its physical relationship is important to the environment, since it has the potential to enhance the religious life of Muslim women in America.

According to the theologian Ibn Hazm (d. 456/1064), the idea of discouraging Muslim women from attending public worship in a mosque came from Abu Hanifa (d. 149/767) and Malik. Ibn Hazm admits that both Abu Hanifa and Malik endorsed the idea that women's prayers in their own houses are better for them. Abu Hanifa allowed elderly women special permission to attend the night (*isha*) prayer and the dawn (*fajr*) prayer, but he did not approve of them attending the two feasts, that is, *Eid al-Adha* and *Eid al-Fitr*.[47] Malik appears to be more cautious, saying, "We do not stop them going out to the mosques and allowing the elderly to attend the feast prayers and the prayer for rain."[48]

Ibn Hazm's mention of these two respectable jurists of the eighth century is understandable. He himself was an exoterist of the Zahiri school of law, which advocates that the only level meaning of the Qur'an is the explicit meaning; according to Ibn Hazm, no hidden meanings are admissible. If we take the term "*masjid*" as it occurs in the Qur'an (for example, in Q. 9:17 and Q. 9:108), the most obvious attribute of the term is that no spatial definition is prescribed. In the twenty-eight or more Qur'anic verses that mention the term "*masjid*," no reference is made to an arrangement based on gender preferences.

There are several ways to deconstruct the legal intent of a mosque, to explain how and why different interpretations of public gathering and gender exist. Since the Qur'an makes no reference to a specific type of ritual space for both men and women, we may start with the seminal mosque, which was constructed on the site where the she-camel knelt upon arrival in Madinah after a long and arduous journey from Makkah (the *hijrah*).

The mosque of the Prophet was used as a public gathering space for male and female companions—the *Muhajirin* (companions/emigrants from Makkah) and the *Ansar* (companions/residents of Madinah). Thus, the *sunnah* of allowing women and men free public access to the mosque was established by explicit approval of the Prophet. The key question that confronts us at this point pertains to a debate that has evolved concerning the right of female worshippers to congregate in public in the mosque. If the Qur'an and the *sunnah* have not set any gender-based limits on the use of the mosque, then why has it become an issue?

Why are women prohibited from attending the mosque even in this day and age? These prohibitions may be the result of cultural stimuli and blind imitation (*taqlid*), or of scholars who are unwilling to, unable to, or uninterested in taking a positive legal position that recognizes the rights of women. Barbara Freyer Stowasser offers a very keen explanation of how architectural stimuli and the revelation of the *hijab* (curtain, partition, or screen) verse concerning privacy may have affected the attitudes of jurists and Muslim interpreters since the time of the Prophet.

Muslim interpreters past and present stipulate that the Prophet's wives participated fully in the communal affairs of Madinah until the revelation of the *hijab* verse. Scholars ascribe their exclusion from public life at that time to several factors. For one, living conditions were extremely crowded, especially in the area around the mosque, which was itself the very center of public activity. It was here that the rooms of the Prophet's wives were located; the rooms stood so close to the mosque that they were a natural extension of the public space (*musallah*). The *hijab* revelation, then, can be understood as a means to provide domestic comfort and privacy for the women.[49]

In the original structure, the nine adjacent apartments, which were used as private domestic quarters in the time of the Prophet, were spatially contiguous with the mosque (*musallah*). The private quarters were entered by way of the *musallah;* it is for this reason that the Qur'anic chapter *surah al-Hujurat,* or "The Inner Apartments," was revealed.

These verses caution the Prophet's companions about "lowering their voices in the presence of Allah's Messenger . . . and refrain[ing] from shouting to the Prophet from outside of the inner apartments" (Q. 49:3–6). The two edifices—the inner apartments and the *musallah*—were separated by a wall with a single door that opened into the *musallah,* dividing the domestic space from the public space. When the Prophet died, he was buried in Ayesha's apartment adjoining the *musallah.* In the rest of the mosque, there were no separated or marked spaces for worship. Stowasser's observations offer insight because she shows how architectural space, etiquette, and privacy are related to revelation and how this relationship was interpreted in the post-Madinah era. The extended corpus of knowledge that we find in the Qur'anic exegesis (*tafsir*) is far too complex to set out in a few paragraphs, especially since the discussion of women in the Qur'an has been addressed extensively by Stowasser. However, it is evident that various interpretations exist. Since most of the authors of these commentaries are men, the explanations of space and gender at each level are presented with a male-oriented vision. The spatial connotation of the *hijab* verse is repeated in various instances, certainly in religious and domestic settings.

Although women often took active part in public life in the early days of Islam, gradually, in later Islamic societies, restrictions often arose. The practice of segregating male and female worshippers in a public place of gathering has been accomplished either with dividing walls in a common space, or with separate spaces.

Thus, different spatial customs have been adopted in different instances. Even with this type of architectural arrangement, some scholars frown upon permitting women to go to the mosque, emphasizing that it is preferable for a woman to pray in her inner apartment. Many of these scholars are aware of the fact that Muslim women offered their prayers in the mosque in the time of the Prophet. Others permit public worship on the condition that a female worshipper must not adorn herself with an excess amount of perfume or use attire that may attract undue attention. These opinions have far-reaching implications with respect to the obligations of worship for men and women; we will return to this discussion below. However, the general agreement of all the major jurists is that the Prophet never stopped the practice of free access; this suggests that in the early Muslim community, women had an unconditional right to attend the mosque.[50]

In a recent survey conducted in Austin, Texas, students interviewed several Muslim women who regularly attend the *masjid* Kadijah bint Khuwaylid, a local mosque named after the first wife of the Prophet.

One woman said that before coming to America, she had never been to a mosque and that, in fact, she did not think the local mosque in her neighborhood back home even had a section for women. She had to move to a non-Muslim country in order to visit a mosque.[51] These remarks are highly perplexing because it is well known that during the time of the Prophet Muhammad, women freely took part in all sorts of religious activities; prayer was not confined to the home.

The best scholarly treatment of this subject is given by S. M. Darsh in a monograph entitled *Islamic Essays* (1979). Darsh cites several well-known scholars—Ibn Hazm, Imam Shawkani, and others—who relate the following two *hadith*s: "Do not prohibit the maid-servants [women] of Allah from coming to the mosques of Allah. When a wife of one of you asks for permission to go to the mosque, she should not be refused permission"; "Do not prevent your women from coming to the mosque, though their houses are better for them."[52]

Another Muslim woman in Austin, Texas, made the following remarks.

Many Muslim [men] do not see any need for a woman to go to a mosque when she can stay at home with the children and pray, even though a mosque may be within a block of her house. In the Prophet's time, women were encouraged to participate fully in the worship life of the community, but over the years this practice has more or less been obliterated. Muslim women in America are more educated and have a chance to be more independent than women in most Muslim countries. American Muslim women, especially of newer generations, are more vocal in demanding equality and equal participation in religious activity.[53]

Her observations confirm the fact that spatial inequality affects the use of public space. The tension that is evident in her remarks reveals a deficiency, which has not been addressed in the legal debate. Despite this deficiency, women in America can join the *Eid* congregational prayer, and they occupy separate rows from the men, as did the women in the time of the Prophet.

American Muslim women understand the significance of public worship. It is a duty and an obligation, and the mosque is generally regarded as a communal gathering space without gender restriction. Today, going to the mosque is a special event, and many people make a family trip out of it.[54] Since the mosque is used for social and educational purposes, it is a place where pious behavior and communal worship are meaningful to belief. Women also understand that the Islamic mode of worship is based on a monotheistic principle (*tauhid*), which admits free and equal right of entry to both men and women. In addition, *tauhid* endorses the belief that Allah is the Single Creator of the universe; therefore, He demands from His creation regular and unrestricted acknowledgment of His sovereignty and dominion (*mulk*). Several Qur'anic verses notify men, women, and jinn (unseen beings created from smokeless fire) concerning the purpose of creation: "I have only created jinn and human beings, that they may worship Me" (Q. 51:56). Another verse encourages traveling and acquiring of knowledge for both men and women: "Travel in the land, and see the nature of the consequence"

(Q. 11:6). Both verses are heuristically useful because they help us to identify the relationship between God and His creation.

The Qur'an further cautions a woman who travels outside her private abode that her attire should cover her entire body, excluding her face, hands, and feet.

> O Prophet! Tell your wives and your daughters and the women of the believers to draw their cloaks [*jalabib*] close round them [when they go outside]. That will be better, so that they may be recognized and not annoyed. Allah is ever Forgiving, Merciful. (Q. 33:59–60)

Based on this verse, many scholars conclude that women are free to go out when necessary, as long as they act upon the verse by concealing the body as described above. They also argue that if women were not permitted to go out and were confined to the home, then the requirement of *hijab* would be meaningless.[55]

In this discussion, I have attempted to address the question of gender and public gathering. Scholarship to date has dealt with a type of mosque architecture in the Muslim world that has been defined formally, spatially, functionally, and temporally. Although prayer in congregation is not obligatory for women, they are not prohibited from offering prayers in the mosque. One final example that supports the argument we have made thus far is the Qur'anic mentions of Mary. In the first mention, whenever Zakariyya entered Mary's prayer niche (*mihrab*), he found she had sustenance that she said was from Allah: "Allah provides sustenance to whom He pleases without measure" (Q. 3:37). In the second mention, Allah commands her to "bow down [in prayer] with those [males] who bow down" (Q. 3:43). Mary is thus asked to pray with the congregation, that is, with the male members of the community.[56] God accepted her service at the temple despite her gender. "Oh Mary! Allah has chosen you and purified you and chosen you over the women of all nations" (Q. 3:42).

Current Western feminist polemics regarding space and gender relationships find their origins in early premodern conceptions of the role of space and the nature of social mannerisms. To document their observations, Western feminist writers approach the subject of environment, geography, and architecture in a related context, writing about the unspoken man–made rules of space and gender.[57] The debate concerning space and gender has engaged the postmodern discourse apropos of architecture and art history, and several works have dealt with various concepts and meanings of gender and space.

In much the same way, contemporary Muslim feminists and historians have studied detailed historical analyses of Muslim communities that emphasize institutional arrangements and political authority; but the debate is almost devoid of spatial connotations and analysis of such issues as the public constraints placed on women in recent times. We have explored the manner in which Muslim scholars have interpreted the spatial arrangement and role of the congregational mosque. My purpose was to suggest how legal perceptions of the mosque differ and why the term "masjid," which occurs in the Qur'an and the hadith, has been the source of so much controversy among historians and scholars in general. In recognition of these societal developments, social scientists and historians have examined the implications regarding, for example, the tradition and theoretical interpretations of Islamic law (shari'ah).

Religious legal paradigms assume that no male or female is exempt from proper behavior when attending public worship in a mosque. Furthermore, every public place of worship has a set of shari'ah rules (ahkam) to determine how it must be used or occupied; these rules can also be viewed as products of related cultural values ('urf).

The question remains: How did later scholars conclude that the mixing of men and women together in a public place for the purpose of worship is prohibited? It is interesting to note once again that the key aspect of the Qur'anic mention of the term "masjid" deals with its spatial sanctity (Q. 72:18) and its physical orientation (Q. 2:149–150). While all of the exegeses of the twenty-eight verses that mention the term "masjid" are crucial to our understanding of the function of a mosque, legal interpretations purport to undertake an inquiry that must address two pivotal assumptions: (1) it is clear from the text of the Qur'an that male and female believers are encouraged to perform regular prayers; and (2) since no gender variables exist in the text of the Qur'an, anyone who enters the space of a masjid is simply required to be in a state of ceremonial purity and to wear proper attire. Apart from these two requirements, there are no other specific criteria for worship.

Understandably, the public and private spatial realms are therefore influenced by nuances of gender and privacy. Since the masjid is a public space, it includes a physical separation of male and female worshippers as well. This practice has become widespread, and it is usually explained as a means of admitting a degree of privacy.

This type of segregation needs to be examined closely, since the spatial conditions that existed in the Prophet's mosque allowed persons of opposite genders to worship in the edifice without any physical or legal restriction.

5. DECONSTRUCTING THE KA'BAH:
The Design Philosophy of a Gathering Space

Professor Latif Khalid Abdulmalik is a New York-born Muslim architect. He supports a design hypothesis for an American mosque—a collective gathering space—that characteristically fuses two types of tropes or philosophical themes.[58] The first one is concerned with the architectural setting of some meaningful quality of space, which is balanced with the idea of a reflective retreat from the material world. The second one recognizes that the mosque—a collective place of prostration—has mixed affiliations, which are spiritual and material. It is for this reason that an architect, when asked to design a religious space, is faced with dual impulses: religious commitment and secular disengagement. In the case of secular disengagement, the object of design is reduced to an academic exercise that too easily dissolves into aesthetic ambiguity and irony. A good example of this approach would be Robert Venturi's design proposal for the Baghdad State Mosque.

> However, in a departure from previous practice, the dome is placed over the *sahn,* an entry courtyard, which provides extra prayer space for as many as 5,000 people. From below, the dome reveals itself as a tree—a huge tree, but light and airy. This great, uplifted double canopy with leaf-like open spaces admits air and sparkling light, preserving the *sahn*'s traditional outdoor character while providing protection from the elements for the people below.[59]

It may be recalled from the introduction that we argued that the spatial qualities of Muslim aesthetics have to do with agreement, accord, and conformity. The dialogue among them is architecture, and the unity and ordering of aesthetics perceived in any outcome is necessarily responsive to each quality. It will be helpful to examine the principles of cubism in light of these remarks. Picasso described cubism as "the manifestation of vague desire . . . to search again for an architectonic basis in the composition, trying to make an order of it."[60] A second interpretation examines the synthetic and analytical aspects of cubism. Many contemporary painters and architects whose work has been influenced by cubism—Peter Eisenman, Michael Graves, Charles Gwathmey, John Hejduk, Richard Meier—follow this line of reasoning to engender their own vocabularies. They adopted a design approach in the late sixties and seventies on the assumption that the cube is entirely understood in Platonic terms. This distinction represents a shift from essence—the essence of African art, upon which cubism is based—toward the straight line, architectural references, and architectural proportions artificially produced. The cubist expression moved architecture in the opposite direction, from its spiritual African origins toward pure Platonic expression. In this sense, "[c]ubism might be thought of as a religious art without religious doctrine."[61] Clearly, the process of using the rationale of synthetic and analytical aspects of design is an artificial one. The individual is absent from the discourse, and the building product is only an object; the object is imitative because it embodies that which is purely creative but rarely reflective. This orientation is expressed more clearly in the following passage.

It [Platonic expression] concerns the plastic and spatial inventions of Cubism and the proposition that whatever may be said about these, they possess an eloquence and a flexibility which continues now to be as overwhelming as it was then. It is an argument largely about the physique of the building and only indirectly about its morale; . . . it should also be envisaged as some sort of interrogation of the mid-twentieth century architect's capacity to indulge his mostly trivial moral enthusiasm at the expense of any physical product.[62]

The result of this type of thinking is a design product that subverts human engagement to absolute imagery; architectural space is largely understood in abstract terms. Abdulmalik's deconstruction of the cube proposes an architectural space that is particularly grounded in a collective understanding of place, space, and time; his approach is both subjective and objective. Subjectively, he considers the spatial features of the Ka'bah—the first cube and *qiblah* and the ontological direction of prayer—important in his architectural formulation because the Ka'bah unites all Muslims to a sacred space, place, and eternal time. According to Muslim tradition, it was Adam who built the Ka'bah, the first cube on earth, and it was later reconstructed by Abraham and Ismail (Q. 2:125–127).

Objectively, a Muslim architect may consider the Ka'bah an architectural metaphor that unites space and time; it also provides the believer with an eschatological connection to human existence.

There exists a meaningful tendency to consider in eschatological terms the psychological insight that the Ka'bah renders, which has also been described by Ibn 'Arabi in his poem "Love Letters to the Ka'ba." For him, it is a place where theophanies (*tajalliyat*) occur. We will return to this discussion below. Objectively, the geometric form of the Ka'bah is inescapable; it conveys a defining character between idea and form and a dynamic architectural proportion that is wholly imaginative. The Sankoré mosque provides an interesting example of how the dimensions of the Ka'bah have been used as a defining theme and an aesthetic reference. This is the only instance of which I am aware where the plan of the Ka'bah was applied to a building in order to develop a valid symbolic prototype. The Sankoré mosque of Mali was originally built by a very rich woman in the northern part of the city of Timbuktu (Tombouctou) in one of the epochs of Tuareg rule; it was rebuilt from the inside out following the return of Qadi el-Aqib from the hajj in 1581.

> Qadi el-Aqib, having ended his pilgrimage, prepared to leave and take the road to Tombouctou, then asked . . . for authorization to determine the number of feet that the Ka'bah measures in length and breadth. Accorded permission, he measured them by means of a cord on which he marked the two dimensions, and then carried this cord to serve as a measure. When he was ready to build the Sankoré mosque, he unrolled the cord and delimited the emplacement by means of four pickets planted on four faces; thus, it had the dimensions of the Ka'bah.[63]

This imaginative use of the dimensions of the Ka'bah has profound psychological consequences for individual believers; one major psychological aspect is the spiritual understanding of believers who come together in the Sankoré to reenact the daily ritual prayer. The aesthetic dimensions of the inner space of the Sankoré mosque are therefore a spiritual reenactment of space and time. The mosque has an entirely metaphorical connotation, especially if we reflect upon Ibn 'Arabi's poem "Love Letters to the Ka'ba," found in his chapter "Crown of Epistles and the Path to Intercessions" (*Taj al-Rasa'il wa-Minhaj al-Wasa'il*).

> Oh Ka'ba of God, oh *Zamzam*, how strongly you demand my friendship, but no, no!
>
> If I must get involved in a friendship with you, it is through compassion and not desire towards you.
>
> The Ka'ba is nothing more than our essence, the essence of curtains of pious fear.
>
> The True One is not contained by sky or earth, or any word.
>
> He appeared to the heart and said to it: Be patient! For it is the *Qiblah* established for Us.
>
> From Us to you and to your hearth, towards the encounter with my house; how magnificent it is.
>
> It is a duty for Our Ka'ba to love you and to love Us is a duty for you.[64]

Describing the respect that Ibn 'Arabi has for the Ka'bah, the lines of the poem contain several metaphorical signs that give rise to a new discourse. Particularly evident in his words is the insistence on obedience, duty, love, compassion, and above all, the existence of God. The reference to containment, a theme that we have explored in the previous discussion, alludes to the *hadith*: "Neither My sky nor My earth contain me; only the heart of My believing servant contains me."[65] In fact, the common denominator in the lines is the sense that the language is both earthly and religious: one cannot escape the fact that the discourse is confined by the paradigm of both subject and object; the experience is therefore internal and external. We will have more to say about the aesthetic implications of this common denominator in the conclusion of this chapter.

Since the aesthetics of postmodern architecture and architecture in general can no longer provide a connection with the spiritual world, the contemporary architect looks outward but not inward in approaching design. Abdulmalik's theory of space provides a relevant debate, which sustains belief as an essential aspect of human existence. Like all believers, Abdulmalik accepts the notion that the Qur'an is the divine revelation from the divine creator, Allah; it is also an eternal guidance to all of creation and the descendants of Adam.

Joseph Ryckwert's *On Adam's House in Paradise* provides a necessary synopsis of an argument similar to this, which attempts to prove that by contributing to an understanding of space and time, the symbol of the house can unify the shared experience of dwelling in all its human dimensions. Christian Norberg-Schulz raises an equally interesting debate in *Existence Space and Architecture*.

Both Ryckwert and Norberg-Schulz propose concepts of space and time that are radically different from those founded on Greek and neo-Platonic models. Since the neo-Platonic model dominates Western thought, design attempts made by Western architects so far have unfortunately not captured or retained the sense of spiritual order based on eschatology.

If the general interpretation of Abdulmalik's tropes or themes leans too heavily toward the metaphysical aspect of form and space, it is a corrective strategy that is meant to rehabilitate the controversy of aesthetics lurking in the minds of postmodern architects and vulnerable clients. Although aesthetic elements do not entirely disappear from Abdulmalik's work, they are effectively taken over by religious and philosophical expectations; hence, eschatology recaptures the essence of time, space, place, and the concrete image of beauty. The first of the two themes that comprise Abdulmalik's design hypothesis deals with his study of cubism and the Ka'bah; the second recognizes an affinity between the text of the Qur'an and aesthetic meaning. Another aspect of his hypothesis lies in the fact that Abdulmalik's interpretations of sacred space and gathering place are mutually reinforcing with regard to the characteristics of contemplation. His definition of space and place must be discussed for at least two reasons:

1. It is meant to take a position on a long-standing controversy about the term "cubism" as it is understood in the West, especially by artists and architects; by making claims to cubism, the Ka'bah has enormous religious and architectural implications.
2. The genesis of Abdulmalik's theory of space and form was formulated while he was still a student at the Cooper Union. His final thesis project was an urban mosque, which we will discuss below.

Abdulmalik describes himself as a cubist because it is a convenient term. His definition of cubism is driven by his study of the proportions of the Ka'bah, so it is not philosophically related to the theories of Juan Gris, Georges Braque, and other advocates of the European cubist movement of the 1920s and '30s. Abdulmalik describes form and space as the "fluid breakup of the cube."[66] He understands form and space to be largely meta-

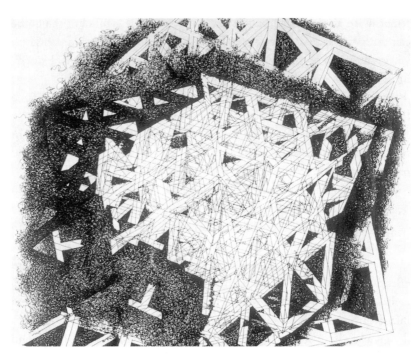

3.13: *Study of the fluid breakup of the cube. Drawing © 1990 by Latif Abdulmalik.*

phorical in their essence and structure. This concept is vastly different from the solutions of Picasso, Braque, and Gris and from the theories that engender the vocabularies of Eisenman, Graves, Gwathmey, Hejduk, and Meier. Again, the subject/object equation is relevant to space and time; to continue with the analogy, Abdulmalik's perception of form and space is fused with light, a parable that also appears in the Qur'an (Q. 24:35). Abdulmalik has commented,

> Each object in space is married to the surface it sits on, and draws energy from the pieces of form adjacent to it. Each object is entitled to its own light and shadow, and its extensions have that same right.[67]

At King Faisal University, Abdulmalik had the students in his course "Form and Geometry" measure the Ka'bah at Makkah; it was during this time that he produced a study entitled *The Force of Space on Form via the Qur'an*. The study, which remains unpublished, is his approach to the arrival of form.

Generally speaking, he reasons that design can be arrived at through some system of thought. Whether formal or abstract, free or limited, it involves a system of thought, which leads to a final design image.[68]

Coming into contact with the physical image and form of the Ka'bah for the first time, he wrote,

> Having gone through something like the general statement (above) [previous excerpt] in college, and having given up the distance that "thought" needs, in exchange for the passion of embodying these words, I have attempted to describe, interpreted configurations, developed in this project using the Qur'an as my reference. These configurations are abstract and based solely on the verses of the Qur'an; and through the experience of being in Makkah. I have touched and seen what I and almost one-fourth of the world believe to be the first cube, built on earth, certainly the existing Ka'bah [cube], which actually measures 11.88 meters × 13.26 meters × 10.25 meters, is no pure cube. . . . There must have been another side or approach to "form," other than existing documentation in relation to Islamic geometric patterns. There must be another answer within the Qur'an itself![69]

Abdulmalik's remarks are significant, and his inclusion of a number of these ideas in the design formula for his thesis at Cooper Union and in the plan of the urban mosque he designed for Harlem is a translation of his theory of space and form. It is based on his acceptance that the Ka'bah is indeed the first cube on earth; the cube is therefore his point of departure. His expectation of the function of space and form and his translation—or rather deconstruction—of the cube remains more difficult to explain.

While Ibn 'Arabi's notions of translation and deconstruction provide an

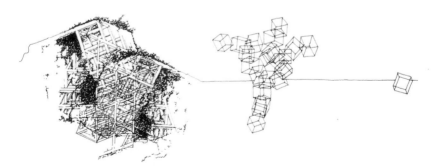

3.14: *Study of the fluid breakup of the cube. Drawing © 1990 by Latif Abdulmalik.*

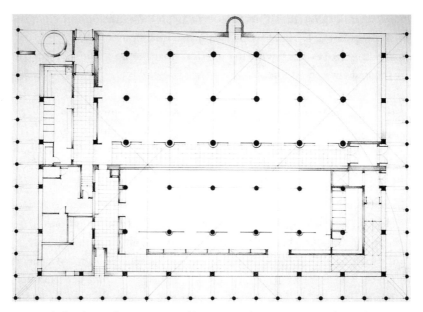

3.15: *Study for a hypostyle mosque in Brooklyn, New York. Drawing © 1998 by Latif Abdulmalik.*

interesting background for understanding more accurately the significance of this approach, an analysis of actual design schemes that explore these ideas is necessary.

Similarly, Abdulmalik's clear rejection of the literal explanation of the common occurrence of geometric patterns in Islamic art and architecture will become clearer to the reader in the course of this discussion.

Abdulmalik's interpretation of cubic order conveys discipline and strength; within its pure form, he sees the cube as fluid when broken down: it must be fluid, since everything is created from water. The breakdown or deconstruction is a means of bringing the state of the pure form to its destination; design in this sense is an innovative effort that captures both image and beauty. Here the notable dichotomies of sections, planes, compression, tension, torsion, and shear are structures that may represent an alternate view of the cubic space. The cube is destroyed without destruction, eliminated without elimination. As Abdulmalik has put it, "Allah wants us to think and use our intellect to represent Him in making beautiful things, whatever they may be."[70]

Interpretation of the written word is another source of Abdulmalik's inspiration. He sees other types of spatial concepts as they are transformed from understanding the text of the Qur'an:

> One day we shall remove the mountains and thou will see the earth as a *level stretch,* and we shall gather them all together nor shall we leave out any one of them. (Q. 18:47; italics mine)

The value of the text assumes an important dimension of eschatological truth, which may be understood in architectural terms as well. It is therefore meaningful to time, form, and space and the symbolic value of four realms of existence—transparent, translucent, reflective, and opaque:

- Life, birth, existence, destiny = transparent realm
- Life on earth, actions recorded = translucent realm
- Life in earth, actions in the grave = reflective realm
- Life after death, resurrection, and judgment = opaque realm

Both linguistic and historical evidence indicates that the above paradigm warrants recognition, since it is a major contribution to the study of design and building production. By the twentieth century, attitudes toward religion may have affected the judgments of artists and architects, especially regarding the correspondences among various ordered hierarchies of religion. If this is the case, the importance of Abdulmalik's thesis is that it helps draw attention to the religious significance of design. His concept of days and the six planes of the cube makes reference to a Qur'anic verse from the chapter "The Heights" (*al-A'raf*): "Your Guardian Lord is Allah, who created the heavens and the earth in six days" (Q. 7:54).

- Day 1 = Paradise/day
- Day 2 = Destiny/existence
- Day 3 = Life on earth, activities recorded
- Day 4 = Life in earth, activities in the grave
- Day 5 = Life after death, resurrection and judgment
- Day 6 = Hell/night

Equally important from the standpoint of aesthetics is the idea that aesthetic sensibilities may vary even in a religious interpretation based on the circle or the cube. Yet the principal idea behind every architectural composition stems from the deletion of space and form in a given context under given conditions; it is therefore the design solution that embodies a certain aim and purpose. But what holds an architectural composition together and what makes it meaningful are entirely different elements. To illustrate what I mean, we have to consider the question of aesthetics. Architecture can include sensory effects, structural effects, functional effects, cultural effects, and a host of other aesthetic concepts, which help define the human and spatial relationships of any composition.

For example, we may recall that most early Renaissance architects experimented with the centralized plan in religious buildings using circles, squares, and domes because such a plan represented for them the absolute geometric essence of man's ontological truth. The aesthetic image of this centralized plan was a well-built man with outstretched arms and feet who fit exactly into the most perfect geometrical figures, circle and square, a criterion that Vitruvius had supplied earlier.

By applying his own rationality and criteria to the study of the Ka'bah, Abdulmalik has introduced a new sense of erudition and originality to the study of religious architecture. But ultimately, the spiritual emotion experienced in a space linked to the Ka'bah, and the response evoked by public devotion and sentiment, identify with religion, history, and spatial traditions.

The aesthetic implications of using the cube as a common denominator include an exploration of the underlying structure of what would otherwise remain a set of dissociated physical phenomena. Abdulmalik's definition of form and space penetrates the human psyche more deeply than the more empirical approach to design might allow. There is a seminal core to his design approach that reveals the underlying significance of human thought, moving thought into form and thus giving meaning to architectural space and experiences.

If the mosque is the product of human assembly, Abdulmalik's schema thus attempts to address the physical phenomenon we call public space. But his framework of public space also admits other types of spiritual phenomena that might have meaning for a large number of people.

Conclusion

REVERSIBLE SPACE
AND LINEAR TIME

Our introductory remarks posited a dynamic relationship between architectural meaning and aesthetic representation by illustrating three major aesthetic genres of Muslim religious architecture in America: syncretic, traditional, and avant-garde. The specific idiom of these particular aesthetic genres is what we have come to call the American mosque. There are several conclusions that can be drawn from the foregoing discussion. Our first conclusion is general; it reasserts our initial hypothesis—which allowed for the precedent of tradition—but with a difference. It acknowledges that no single authoritative aesthetic tradition exists in Islam that can be individually claimed by any community. Instead, what we find is an authoritative adherence to a litany of aesthetic principles that are common to dogma and religious practice among Muslims.

This common occurrence finds its origins in the principles of Islamic monotheism, or *tauhid,* which has been offered as an explanation for the aesthetic relationship of unity in diversity in Muslim art and architecture. Writing about *tauhid* and aesthetics in a seminal essay called *Tawhid [Tauhid]: Its Implications for Thought and Life,* the late professor Ismail al-Farouqi says that

> *Tawhid* means the ontological separation of the Godhead from the whole realm of nature. Everything that is in or of creation is a creature, nontranscendent, subject to the laws of space and time. Nothing of it can be God or Godly in any sense, especially the ontological which *tawhid,* as the essence of monotheism, denies. . . .
>
> It is idle to dispute the unity of Islamic art. Although the historian will recognize a large variety of motifs, of materials, of styles differentiated

geographically or chronologically, the overwhelming fact of all Islamic art is its unity of purpose and form. All Islamic art has recourse to and used the highly emotive words of the Qur'an and the *hadith,* of Arabic or Persian poetry or of the Islamic wisdom literature. . . . In such cases, their distinctive reason and understanding were not at work, but their sensory and intuitive faculties went into full play, apprehending the aesthetic values in evidence. Such was the power of the aesthetic values of Islam and such was the artistic unity they produced out of the most diverse assemblage of cultures.[1]

I have referred to the term *"tauhid"* in the introduction and elsewhere as the aesthetics of monotheism. *Tauhid* affects the use of imagery and iconography in religious aesthetics; above all, it is a monotheistic concept of beauty, which calls for a detachment from the anthropomorphic world, its reflection, or its representation.[2] In extant examples of Muslim religious architecture, the characteristics of unity in diversity can be found in a variety of regional styles. Unity is created order that is based on ecological harmony, cosmology, and balance (*wazn*). Diversity allows for the inclusion of cultural nuances and the accommodation of regional styles, which do not upset the balance but give it greater depth. A diversity of styles has flourished since the eighth century C.E., along with the formative development of the congregational mosque, the adoption of various building conventions, and the use of specific types of local building materials. Examples of regional styles survive in the Middle East, North, East, and West Africa, central Asia, South Asia, the Far East, and many peripheral communities.

In light of this historical fact, we may speak of Muslim religious aesthetics as having three direct qualifying factors with regard to any given style or expression, which are: normative, generative, and adaptive. These three qualifying factors are useful because they address the nuances of culture, geography, and environment. In addition, they are useful in identifying the development of a style or an expression. They have shaped the stylistic features of mosques away from the center of origin, that is, in places outside of Arabia, the birthplace of Islam. Finally, normative, generative, and adaptive themes represent an important aesthetic treatment and a valid statement in the perception of a local community, an architect, a builder, or a patron.

In our aesthetic evaluation of the American mosque, we have cited several examples to demonstrate the nuances of each of the aforementioned factors; however, a further note of clarity is essential. Because physical setting and linear time differ, religious aesthetics and the art of space making are affected by the peculiarities of a local history or the collective knowledge of a community. With regard to the American mosque, linear time and the art of space making are further problematic for two key historical reasons: (1) there is no documented architectural chronology apropos of the historical development of Muslim religious aesthetics in North America that dates to the antebellum era, when the first community of Muslims from West Africa was enslaved in America; and (2) similarly, there are no extant Muslim religious structures that date to the same period.[3] In spite of this historical discontinuity, it is possible to reconstruct the image of an antebellum mosque based on the wealth of written documents left behind that have been recently studied. Because of the excellent research work done by Sylviane Diouf and other scholars, we now have a fairly accurate knowledge of how the Muslim slaves worshipped during their period of captivity.[4]

When West African Muslim slaves were first brought to America in the sixteenth century C.E., there was no possible opportunity to construct any type of religious building. Therefore, a major structure depicting an identifiable ethnic or regional expression, linked to architectural traditions of West Africa, did not exist. The reason for this religious anomaly is well understood. The American Muslim slave community, although very devout, was hindered by the subjugation and inhuman treatment of slavery and by the restrictions placed on religious practice in general among slaves. Furthermore, archaeological evidence that can identify sites where mosques were possibly built in the antebellum period has yet to be discovered. Because of this architectural discontinuity, several writers have erroneously stated that the so-called mother mosque of Cedar Rapids, Iowa, (built in 1934) is the oldest extant Muslim religious structure in North America. But after all, how do we define a mosque (*masjid*)? We have debated the hermeneutics of the term "*masjid*" at length in chapter 1. In keeping with the *hadith* that states "the [whole] earth is a *masjid*," an antebellum mosque may have been a rudimentary building, quite temporary and unrefined; and in some instances, a simple demarcated space on the ground—under the dome of the sky—facing Makkah would have sufficed without an enclosed structure.

In spite of the chronological discontinuity that exists in architectural history between medieval West Africa and antebellum North America, these remarks say something about the presence of Islam in America prior to emancipation in 1865. In recognition of that presence, a mosque in Fayette-ville, North Carolina, is named after a well-known West African Muslim slave and scholar, Omar Ibn Sayyid (d. 1865). After 1865, religious buildings began to appear in Ross, North Dakota (1929); Cedar Rapids, Iowa (1934); and Pittsburgh, Pennsylvania (1928). Long before the arrival of Muslim im-migrants in the 1930s—from the Middle East, the Indian subcontinent, and other parts of the Muslim world—there was a significant Muslim presence in North America. Today the American Muslim community claims six to eight million adherents and is a mosaic of sixty or more ethnic groups. The predominant ethnic group, African American orthodox (Sunni) Mus-lims, represents 45 percent of the North American community. According to some accounts, there are over three thousand mosques in America; many of these are converted structures or storefront buildings.[5] In spite of these numbers, the stylistic features of the West African mosque have not re-gained acceptance in North America. One explanation has to do with the lack of scholastic recognition for the West African mosque. Labelle Prussin has dealt with the topic quite thoroughly in her book *Hatumere: Islamic De-sign in West Africa.* Her work has clearly demonstrated that the West African mosque is a legitimate style, contradicting most art historians, who have exercised extreme bias by ignoring this fact.[6]

By the sixteenth century C.E., West Africa had long been established as a cultural and economic entrepôt, since Islam had gained a foothold in the re-gion in the tenth century.[7] Well-established traditions of Muslim religious architecture and art have been in existence since that time, and certainly, by literary accounts, they were firmly in place by the fourteenth century C.E., when Mansa Musa made his famous pilgrimage to Makkah.

Our second conclusion calls attention to a formidable dichotomy: when a community migrates, do aesthetic traditions change countries with it as well? Since we have argued that the American mosque is a mosque away from the center of origin, its hybrid expression may account for its lack of scholastic attention. Nevertheless, it represents an aesthetic image, which the diaspora community in America may regard with high esteem. The problems that we found with the use of an architectural image to signify aesthetic identity and space making were adequately discussed in chapter 2. A critique of image making, space making, and aesthetic meaning and a proper analysis of the historical and cultural nuances were also undertaken in chapters 2 and 3.

Because of the deep respect for cultural identity in the diaspora community, I would like to propose yet another idiom to explain the importance of cultural identity. We may invoke the idiom "ethnocentric expression" because it suggests a dominant genre in the development of ethnic expression by a Muslim community on the periphery, that is, in a strange land and away from its origin. Readers interested in pursuing this discussion and the forms of cultural representation related to it can explore the work of Barbara Daly Metcalf in *Making Muslim Space in North America and Europe* and Kathleen M. Moore in *Al-Mughtaribun*.[8] In a parallel analysis, Robert Mugerauer's *Interpreting Environments: Tradition, Deconstruction, Hermeneutics* explores various modalities of environment and ways to deconstruct various types of structures, landscapes, and images.

As I have stated above, the American mosque is a neoteric architectural genre; therefore, any immature aesthetic tendency will demonstrate a variety of stylistic dichotomies. By invoking the idiom "ethnocentric expression," we address one type of dichotomy, which identifies the visual complexities of a structure. Furthermore, each type of visual complexity is predicated on a self-conscious choice or depiction of an architectural image. The idiom "ethnocentric expression" emphasizes the visual aspect, but it informs an interdisciplinary discourse, which makes claims about architectural meaning, identity, and design. The design process is complex because it can propose either an ingenious design solution or a set of new aesthetic problems. I have noted the example of the Islamic Institute of Boston because, based on my evaluation, it is an ingenious design solution that has dealt with the problem of architectural meaning and image.

Returning to the question of architectural meaning, identity, and design, the first problem concerns the self-conscious space-making processes that we find in a non-Muslim environment such as North America. This problem proposes an interesting challenge to any architect. What happens when a culture is displaced and is forced to create images and themes to re-represent itself elsewhere? How is it possible to create a genuine ethnocentric expression with such a diverse community? One possible response to these questions is addressed by a third question. Can design principles embody cultural meaning, or are they the reason why it is so difficult to understand design complexity? The decision an architect faces when having to justify the use of an image is akin to spatial identity and aesthetic expression. Any design criteria related to these three may suggest an interesting path of knowledge towards understanding an ethnocentric expression. Given these complexities, we have studied the aesthetic language of the American mosque as if it were a displaced or migrant model, in order to explain why and how it is imbued with various cultural mannerisms.

The key to understanding the aesthetic language of a community on the periphery is a focus aside from the concerns of linear time, which we have already discussed, and away from the concept of center. To study the community on the periphery, I have proposed a theoretical model of deconstruction. In the introduction, I proposed a method of deconstruction using Ibn 'Arabi's notions of subject and object. This model is likely to provoke, rather than alter, the attitude of an art historian, because this emphasis proposes a philosophical inquiry, which in my view helps to explain aesthetic ambiguity or architectural theory.

Our third conclusion outlines why I have used the term "peripheral model" to describe the American mosque. The reason concerns various types of design inferences resulting from the manipulation of the design process. Take for example the following synopsis: A decision maker, the building committee, the patron, or the community can be held accountable for selecting a style from among a litany of regional styles. That style is then imposed upon an architect during the stage of design development. For example, SOM, designer of the Islamic Cultural Center of New York (in Manhattan), complained about the attempts at manipulation that came from two camps: camp A, the traditionalists, who advocated a rigorous use of imagery, and camp B, the modernists, who supported an avant-garde expression. The end result of whose decision prevails during the design process varies from case to case; nevertheless, it is a complicated process, which entails a dialectic argument between tradition and modernity. There are shortcomings on both sides of the argument. For example, a traditional style may be predicated on limited knowledge of history or may reflect a cultural bias. And modern style may embrace design technology or embody emerging trends in the field of architecture that ignore history. Ultimately, any style must display a functional understanding of environment and a conventional knowledge of appropriate building codes, construction norms, and other environmental regulations. The vast majority of mosques built in America over the past fifty years have demonstrated one or more of these conditions. Returning to the problem of manipulation during the design process, consider what Professor Gulzar Haider has to say about the harsh reality of dealing with a mosque planning committee.

I have wandered far and wide in landscapes of Muslim diaspora in search of opportunities to serve. With youthful idealism blunted, and time asserting its ruthless compulsion to move, I offered myself, with transparent eagerness, to design mosques for Muslims in the West. Repeatedly, I get seduced by the mosque committees promising me credit in the life "hereafter" and end up in painfully one-sided, almost exploitative contracts in this life "here." A scream remains muffled in my chest, and I am afraid that if it ever escapes it will startle the angels. As a designer meeting my clients, I find myself imprisoned in a cell with comatose *imam*s, deaf firebrands, blind guides and unemployable volunteers. With some strange resilience I have walked into many such cells across North America, but the same macabre actors are ahead of me to stage the same mad show all over again.[9]

In response to the decision of a committee, designers and architects have generally had to deal with a host of aesthetic anomalies and ethnic preferences that are likely, in the long run, not to solve but to create a host of other design problems. Professor Haider believes that such problems may stem from the fact that

Muslims in the non-Islamic West are undoubtedly grounded but not yet rooted. Theirs is a promising exile: a freedom of thought, action and inquiry that is unknown in the contemporary Muslim world. They are challenged by a milieu that takes pride in oppositional provocations.[10]

It is not impossible to overcome these difficult design challenges, but it is clear that architects require a superior degree of communicative skills and an unlimited amount of patience when dealing with committees that are religiously or culturally charged. Basic architectural knowledge is not enough, although it is crucial to the design process. It is also necessary that the designer and the client be able to understand real-world settings to avoid piecemeal or impaired design solutions. Commenting about the current practice of architecture among Muslim architects, Professor Oleg Grabar has observed that there is little doubt that

In recent years, however, a more interesting and more creative trend has made its appearance among designers. Several impulses affect it. One is that, as extensive building programs acquire a style instead of being ready-made imports of soulless tool kits, the mosque needs to be fitted within an over-all system of formal ideas. Another one is the effect of post-modernism and paramodernism; greater freedom of formal expression has affected most traditional and set ways and the mosques, it is felt, can be liberated from the constraints of the past. A third impulse affects primarily Muslim architects who seek to find new but acceptable forms for this most uniquely Muslim function.[11]

Judging from the design proposals and completed projects I have studied over the last two decades, I believe that Grabar's argument is laudable. It is for this reason that I discussed the major aesthetic premises employed in each design case mentioned above; my intention was to demonstrate or to discover the salient aspects of Muslim architecture and the meanings of beauty (*jamal*) and aesthetic truth. But we may add to Grabar's remarks that in North America, there is a litany of complex impulses that affect Muslim and non-Muslim architects who seek to find new and acceptable forms of expression "for this most uniquely [simple] Muslim function."[12] We have noted in the introduction how Ibn 'Arabi argued that the architect (*arbab al-Handasah*) is an authorized agent of creativity and how creativity and its resulting object can demonstrate patterns of subjectivity, objectivity, and beauty. One may ask whether the phenomenological and psychological relationship among subject, object, form, image, and beauty is entirely aesthetic or metaphorical. From our discussion of Professor Abdulmalik's aesthetic theory of subject, object, form, image, and beauty, a phenomenological and psychological relationship can be understood. His deconstruction conceives of the Ka'bah as a specific form and image and, likewise, a beautiful object. The same type of reasoning applies to the properties of phenomenologi-cal and psychological relationships that we discover in the aesthetics of the American mosque.

That said, we must stress how likely it is that the etymology of the term "aesthetics" (Gk. *aisthetikos*), seemingly endemic to the practice of architec-ture, is replete with complexities and contradictions. Add to this the claim that the noun *aisthetika*, literally translated as "aesthetics" in English, origi-nally meant "sensory perception" or "the science of poetics."[13] These two etymologies may be characterized as having their source in a religious para-digm. Our discussion of Hassan Fathy's Dar al-Islam project was intended to illustrate this point; likewise, our discussion of El-Wakil's Muslim Center of Miami dealt with the nature of a space created for spiritual repose.

Speaking about the nature of a religious space, Le Corbusier made some poignant remarks, when he visited the mosques of Istanbul, that call our attention to the spiritual aspects of a term used by Claude Levi-Strauss for alternating cyclical time: "reversible space and linear time."[14] Le Corbusier's mention of the collective act of repeated submission (*sajda*) appears right along with his discussion of the space of Ottoman mosques in Istanbul. This experience involves a man-made space, regulated by the sun, and the human voice, which calls the faithful to prayer. He describes a pious moment of worship, regulated by the call to prayer, in order to draw our attention to the architectural relationship of various spatial elements that are sympathetic to space and time.

> Flanking the sanctuary, there must be minarets so tall as to carry afar the shrill voices of the muezzins chanting and calling the devoted to prayer at hours regulated by the sun. Impressive notes filter down from above. . . . Within its own city of stones, the white sanctuary raises its dome atop great cubes of masonry. An elementary geometry orders these masses: the square, the circle, the cube, the sphere. In plan it is a rectangular complex with a single axis. The orientation of the axis of every mosque on Muslim soil toward the black stone of the *Ka'bah* is an awe-inspiring symbol of unity of the faith. . . . Bare-footed, the faithful line up in various places in the nave and prostrate often, all together. Having waited for long-lasting seconds with heads bowed to the ground, then upright with heads beholding the *mihrab* and hands folded in worship, they would repeat "Allah," in a deep voice after the *imam*'s utterance from the gallery.[15]

These remarks fuse two genres of reversible space and linear time by way of analogy. The first is a ritual enactment—a daily recurrence of communal worship—related to the normative configuration of the first communal space built in the seventh century C.E. The second type of experience is one that orients the worshipper in space and time: the *mihrab* and its ontological axis. Is Le Corbusier endorsing our claim that a sacred space can only exist in relation to the human acts of piety, which also require space and time?

Toward the end of the time I spent writing this book, I received an essay from Rabia Van Hattum entitled "Ranchos Mosque: A Memoir." Rabia resides at Abiquiu, New Mexico. Her husband, Benyamin, is a highly skilled and experienced wood craftsman and builder, very adept with joinery and tile work; and Rabia is an accomplished musician and a mother. Rabia's memoir about the building of a little white mosque is a poignant explanation of the piety, love, labor, and generosity that made this twenty-five-by-fifteen-foot building possible. Above all, Rabia's reflection is a positive attitude that observes the righteousness that the Qur'an enjoins between Muslim men and women. Rabia writes,

> I'm [reminded of] when we raised the Ranchos mosque. The hearts of all the creatures are between our lord's hands, and it is He alone who can cause goodness or other than goodness to grow there. . . . It was our hope that establishing a mosque would bring us together in prayer, and that our Lord would be pleased with us all for overcoming the divergence in our neighborhood. . . . Benyamin chose the site. He paced it out and located the *qiblah* and began digging the trenches. . . . I remember what a pure and joyous spirit existed amongst the men that day. *Alhamdulillah* [All praise is due to Allah], it's rare to witness that kind of love and light in brotherhood, shining so distinctly, so uninhibitedly.[16]

Rabia's reading of the mosque is made meaningful in contemporary eyes by the fact that it is written about the religious experience of Muslim men and women. The same point was made about the building of the Prophet's mosque, which was at the core of the Madinah community. It allowed Muslim men and women to build a community together and to worship together; this effect transfers most immediately to Rabia's narrative.

Rabia makes a number of other impressive remarks about the Ranchos mosque, but in principle, she explains her personal satisfaction and the satisfaction of others at the completion of the Ranchos mosque.

> The mosque has provided shelter for all kinds of Muslim travelers: conservative and eccentric, foreign and home-grown. We've had some good times with our children there too: reading and listening to tales of the prophets, coloring Islamic designs, attempting to learn Arabic, drawing on the chalkboard. The best times now are when we gather for *dhikr* [remembrance of God]. Allah is not concerned with our outer forms, but is always mindful of the state of our hearts. I am so grateful for every opportunity to sit with the lovers of Allah, remembering Him, reciting His holy names and attributes, glorifying Him, praising Him. It is in that circle that we can taste our salvation.[17]

4.1: *Ranchos mosque, Abiquiu, New Mexico. Photograph © 2000 by Ronald Baker. Courtesy of Ronald Baker.*

We need to consider the allegory of time and space against Rabia's luminous remarks. Space and time may be understood as a continuum that extends from the very common attributes of the *sunnah,* a narrative and exemplary code of human behavior that owes its testimony to the Prophet Muhammad. We have put forward the concept of spatial *sunnah* in chapter 1 because it is as pertinent today as it was in seventh-century Arabia. Citing the spatial *sunnah* as an architectural convention has led to another discussion: space and gender.

The collision of space and gender is arguably an inversion of the spatial arrangement that the *sunnah* sanctions.

In chapter 3, I suggested ways in which the spatial *sunnah* has become distorted by undue cultural or religious bias, in particular in instances of spatial confrontation or masculine conventions.

Our final consideration in this conclusion is Jaan Holt's representation of the properties of a gathering space, which raises the issue of public gathering. His is a rudimentary attempt to suggest that the structure of a mosque is very much a part of collective agreement (*ijma*) and that it is indeed human agreement that matters most. He offers an intriguing analogy beyond the contradictions of history and the limitations of an established space for wor-

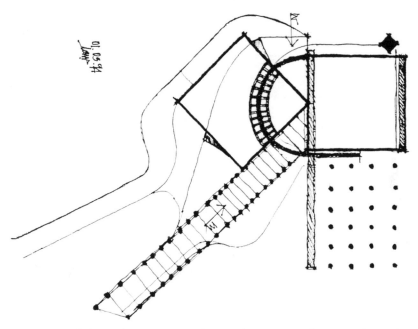

4.2: *Design study for an urban mosque in Harlem, Manhattan, New York. Drawing © 1994 by Latif Abdulmalik.*

ship. He defines the agreed space simply as "the wall facing Mecca," a phrase that he uses as the title of an essay and of the following poem.

> Before the presence of the wall.
> Architecture could be thought of as the material room approaching the
>   spiritual room through the realm of human agreement.
> In the act of prayer, the material room is not there, not even the floor is
>   there; really, not even the carpet, which is the ordained surface of the
>   paradise garden, is quite there.
> Only the act in its attitude is wholly there.[18]

What is most intriguing about Holt's characterization of "the wall facing Mecca" is that a wall represents an outer edge of any gathering space or enclosure.

This remark holds true for the concept of form as well. If we recall the previous discussion, the sacred space integrates both material and spiritual requirements, but it also requires the presence of the faithful.

In Holt's scheme, a sacred space is defined by a self-regulating wall facing

Makkah [Mecca]. The wall is autonomous; it is capable of transformation; and it is free of all aesthetic exigencies except that it must observe the axis of prayer. But above all, Holt's definition of a gathering space is motivated by human agreement. This has been my view as well. In my critique of the American mosque, I have dealt with the themes of space, gender, and aesthetics in light of four primary architectural considerations: (1) the ideal and informal qualities of a mosque, which is essentially a religious gathering space; (2) the American mosque as work of art and architecture and its physical environment; (3) the conceptual juxtaposition of functional, aesthetic, and material considerations; and (4) the textual, emotional, and intellectual power of deconstruction using Ibn 'Arabi's notion of subject and object.

The validity of this approach and of the method of deconstruction employed is grounded in the belief that a contextual reading of the American

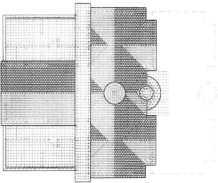

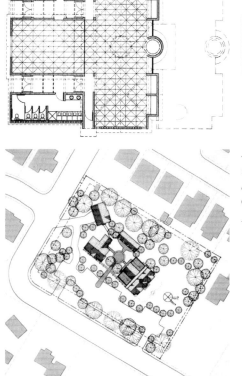

4.3 (a–c): *Design study for an urban mosque in Austin, Texas. Craig Anz, architect, in collaboration with Akel Ismail Kahera. Drawing © 2000 by I'M Architects (Integrated Metropolis).*

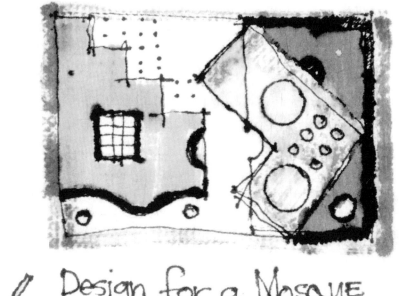

4.4: *Design study for a neighborhood mosque in Newark, New Jersey. Drawing © 1983 by Akel Ismail Kahera.*

mosque involves nuances of human agreement. And because of the strong affinity that the practice of Islam holds for a diverse community in this distinct North American environment, such nuances cannot be ignored. Finally, we need only to consider Holt's remarks once more, since they strengthen our notion of human agreement.

But since Holt's spatial conception is wholly rational, the real justification for the existence of the gathering space that we have called the American mosque can only be found in the spiritual and physical presence of the edifice itself.

> The wall facing Mecca is the place of human agreement [*ijma*] to prayer. In its making, it attests to this sense of agreement, and allows an individual the same freedom from reproach as if he/she were alone; yet it affords through architecture the generosity of the presence of many.[19]

Holt's remarks seem to suggest that consensus (*ijma*), not discord, is capable of providing the inspiration for aesthetic comprehensibility. If we explore this reasoning further, it is possible that the petition for *ijma* is meant to rescue the client/end user from selfishness, and the architect from the pitfalls of mediocrity, by yielding vigorous and responsible solutions that corroborate the aesthetics of monotheism.

With this idea in mind, we can think of the American mosque as an edifice that deserves aesthetic attention, if only because it reminds us of the visual difficulties and conflicts inherent in religious architecture and art. That is why the aim of this book has been to introduce a fresh debate about a familiar religious edifice, in conjunction with a study of the particularities of space, gender, and aesthetics.

And finally, I would say that the aesthetic prejudices that continue to cloud many people's understanding of these particularities—by virtue of the direct correspondence to the character of the American Muslim community—could eventually become less of an obstacle. *Ijma* provides a means of escape from the narrow understanding of environment and the interpretation of knowledge. It is for this reason that Holt's assertion is worth consideration; the power of human agreement has the ability to transform each individual.

This makes the American mosque an important religious edifice because in its evolution, it will continue to provide a place for spiritual repose and public gathering. Above all, its enduring presence confirms the obligation to enact communal worship, and the essentiality of observing the primordial value of public gathering in Islam.

NOTES

INTRODUCTION

1. For example, see Adib Nayif Diyab, "Intellect and Imagination in Ibn 'Arabi's Anthropological Epistemology."

2. Kathleen M. Moore, *Al-Mughtaribun [Emigrants]: American Law and the Transformation of Muslim Life in the United States,* esp. 117–133.

3. Aminah Beverly McCloud, *African American Islam,* esp. 135–159.

4. For example, see the following essays: Akel Kahera, "Visual and Religious Arts"; Akel Kahera, "Image, Text and Form: Complexities of Aesthetics in an American Masjid"; Omar Khalidi, "Approaches to Mosque Design in North America"; Gulzar Haider, "Brother in Islam, Please Draw Us a Mosque: Muslims in the West: A Personal Account."

5. Barbara Daly Metcalf, *Making Muslim Space in North America and Europe,* 21.

6. Ibid.

7. For a detailed summary of the Muslim population in the United States as of 1992, see Fareed H. Numan, "The Muslim Population In The United States: A Brief Statement." According to Numan's data, among Muslims in the United States, African Americans comprise 42% of the total; 24.4% are South Asians; 12.4% are Arabs; 5.2% are Africans; 3.6% are Iranians; 2.4% are Turks; 2% are Southeast Asians; 1.6% are White Americans; 0.8% are eastern Europeans; and all other groups comprise 5.6%. The ten states with the highest numbers of Muslims are California, New York, Illinois, New Jersey, Indiana, Michigan, Virginia, Texas, Ohio, and Maryland (listed in descending order of Muslim population). These ten states together represent 3.3 million Muslims. In 1992 there were more than 1,500 mosques, compared to 600 in 1980, 230 in 1960, and 19 in 1930. In addition, there were 400 Islamic schools (108 full time), over 400 associations, an estimated 200,000 businesses, and over 80 publications, journals, weekly newspapers, etc.

8. Dora P. Crouch and June G. Johnson, *Traditions in Architecture,* 3.

9. The first mosque built at Madinah, chronologically, is the Kuba mosque.

I am referring to the Prophet's mosque, which is mentioned explicitly in the *hadith*.

10. Here I use the term *"sunnah"* to suggest the mannerisms, sayings, practices, and moral example of the Prophet Muhammad (d. 632 C.E.).

11. Diyab, "Intellect and Imagination."

12. Akel Ismail Kahera, "The Architecture of the West African Mosque: An Exegesis of the Hausa and Fulani Models."

13. I have discussed this problem elsewhere. See Akel Kahera and Gulshah Yildirim, "The Site Where the She-Camel Knelt Down: Exegesis, Gender and the Public Domain."

14. Secular buildings in the Middle East have to confront the same dilemma. See the discussion of this problem in Akel Kahera, "ENPPI Headquarters Building, Cairo, Egypt."

15. Robert Venturi, *Complexity and Contradiction in Architecture.*

16. See Mildred Fischmertz, "Mosque as Monument."

17. When architects from the West were invited to design a state mosque for Baghdad in 1982, the majority of the entries were heavily grounded in a secular world of ideas and interpretation: highly experimental, liberal, pluralistic, and dispossessed.

18. See Sylviane A. Diouf, *Servants of Allah: African Muslims Enslaved in the Americas.*

19. Le Corbusier, *Journey to the East,* 94–95.

20. John Burchard and Albert Bush-Brown, *The Architecture of America,* 3.

21. Metcalf, *Making Muslim Space,* 31–46.

CHAPTER ONE

1. Since it is often helpful to start with a conventional account of the meaning of the term *"masjid"* (mosque), this chapter will seek to clarify and assess the implications of the word. I use the terms "mosque" and *"masjid"* interchangeably throughout this essay.

2. Oleg Grabar, "Symbols and Signs in Islamic Architecture," 3.

3. Ibid., 1.

4. For an excellent essay on the study of form, see Abraham Edel and Jean Francksen, "Form: A Philosophic Idea and Some of Its Problems."

5. Robert Mugerauer, *Interpreting Environments: Tradition, Deconstruction, Hermeneutics,* xxvi.

6. For example, see Ghazi Bisheh, "The Mosque of the Prophet at Madinah throughout the First Century A.H."

7. See Kahera, "Image, Text and Form: Complexities of Aesthetics in an American Masjid."

8. The reference to congregational worship occurs in Q. 62:9–10.

9. The Prophet prayed facing Bait al-Maqdis (Jerusalem) for sixteen or seventeen months until the following verses were revealed: "Verily, We have seen the

turning of your face to the heaven!" (Q. 2:144); "Say: 'To Allah belongs the East and the West. He guides whom He will to a straight path'" (Q. 2:142).

10. This problem is briefly discussed in my essay "ENPPI Headquarters Building, Cairo, Egypt." For over two decades, in my own research and design practice in the Middle East, I have investigated the use of form-making codes, for instance, in the design of a religious edifice. I have found that they provide a useful means of codifying or correlating information when dealing with design problems that are apropos of a distinct cultural or religious context.

11. *Sahih al-Bukhari,* vol. 1, book 7, no. 331.

12. See Q. 2:22.

13. Several Qur'anic verses cite the term. For example: "And the places of worship [*masajid*] are for Allah [alone]: So invoke not anyone along with Allah" (Q. 72:18); "It is not for such as join gods with Allah, to visit or maintain [to build or repair] the mosques [*masajid*] of Allah while they witness against their own souls to infidelity. The works of such bear no fruit: In fire shall they dwell" (Q. 9:17).

14. *Sahih Muslim,* vol. 1, no. 1068.

15. The *qiblah* is universally recognized by its *mihrab,* which signifies the point where, facing Makkah, the *imam* stands, leading the faithful in prayer.

16. An individual worshipper in an outdoor open field must also face Makkah. The act and the intention are prima facie states of belief and devotion.

17. Iconography is consciously absent from the aesthetic features of *masjid* architecture, since it constitutes a principal agent of polytheism (*shirk*), which is a gross violation of the principle of the unity and oneness of Allah (*tauhid*). *Masajid* throughout the world adhere to this aesthetic principle.

18. *Sahih al-Bukhari,* vol. 1, no. 437.

19. Nur al-Din al-Samhudi, *Wafa al-Wafa,* 334–346. Al-Samhudi explains the cubit (*dhirar*) as two hand spans (*shibran*). The conventional measurement of the cubit is the distance from the elbow to the tip of the middle finger, or approximately 17.4 to 20.64 inches (*Webster's Collegiate Dictionary,* 2nd ed., s.v. "cubit"). It would appear that the cubit varies from country to country and among builders. The first building of the Prophet's mosque reportedly measured some sixty cubits by seventy cubits; these measurements differ among various historical accounts (see al-Samhudi, 334–336). Al-Samhudi notes several reports concerning the measurement of the building: sixty by seventy cubits; one hundred by one hundred cubits; and less than one hundred cubits. The building was subsequently expanded on several occasions. The first major expansion (C.E. 708–711) occurred during the period of the caliph al-Walid ibn Abdul Malik, who ordered the governor of Madinah, Umar ibn Abdul Aziz, to renovate the mosque. Apparently, the first minarets were added during the time of Umar ibn Abdul Aziz.

20. See Q. 2:137–147.

21. This poem was first cited in Ibn Ishaq, *Sirat,* 3–4:666–669. The first English version appears in the translation rendered by A. Guillaume, *The Life of Muhammad: A Translation of Ishaq's* Sirat Rasul Allah, 795–798. The version I cite here is from Juan Eduardo Campo, *The Other Sides of Paradise,* 56. I have included the second-

to-last line as it appears in Ghazi Bisheh's "The Mosque of the Prophet at Madinah throughout the First Century A.H." The line does not appear in Campo.

22. "The predominant meaning of the *Sunnah* is that of the spoken and acted example of the Prophet. It includes what he approved, allowed, or condoned." *The Concise Encyclopaedia of Islam,* 1st. ed., s.v. "Sunnah."

23. I am referring here again to Nur al-Din al-Samhudi's *Wafa al-Wafa.* This is perhaps the most authoritative text on the early history of Madinah.

24. Paul Sebag, *The Great Mosque of Kairouan,* 103.

25. Alan Leary, "The Development of Islamic Architecture in the Western Sudan," 22.

26. P. F. Stevens, *Aspects of Muslim Architecture in the Dyula Region of the Western Sudan,* 38.

27. Kathryn L. Green, "Dyula and Sonongui in the Region of Kong," 100.

28. Ibid., 103.

29. The Prophet's mosque was built of mud bricks and date trees used as columns and roof supports. See *Sahih Muslim,* vol. 1, no. 266.

30. This argument has been put forward by Labelle Prussin. See *Hatumere: Islamic Design in West Africa.*

31. Rene Bravmann, *Islam and Tribal Arts in West Africa,* 29–31.

32. Susan McIntosh and Roderick McIntosh, "The 1981 Field Season at Jenne-Jenno: Preliminary Results," 31.

33. See Roderick McIntosh, "Square Huts in Round Concepts: Prediction of Settlement Features in West Africa."

34. For a detailed study of the art and architectural styles that were brought to the New World from Spain, see T. B. Irving, *Mudejar Crafts in the Americas.*

35. Roger Kennedy, *Mission: The History of the Missions of North America,* 56.

36. George Kubler, *Religious Architecture of Mexico in the Colonial Period and Since the American Occupation,* 75.

37. See Thomas Drain, *A Sense of Mission: Historic Churches of the Southwest,* 4.

38. See Rex Newcomb, *The Franciscan Mission Architecture of Alta California,* 47.

39. Kennedy, *Mission,* 74.

40. Ibid., 96.

41. James Early, *The Colonial Architecture of Mexico,* 118–119.

42. Trent Sandford, *The Story of Mexican Architecture,* 146.

43. T. B. Irving, *Mudejar Crafts in the Americas,* 11.

44. Gerald Bernstein, "In Pursuit of the Exotic: Islamic Forms in Nineteenth-Century American Architecture," 92.

45. Ibid.

46. Ibid., 95.

47. Leon A. Jick, *The Americanization of the Jewish Synagogue.*

48. Bernstein, "In Pursuit of the Exotic," 110; Jick, *The Americanization of the Jewish Synagogue,* 183.

49. Bernstein, "In Pursuit of the Exotic," 111.

50. Jick, *The Americanization of the Jewish Synagogue,* 179.

51. Bernstein, "In Pursuit of the Exotic," 150.

52. Ignacio San Martin, ed., *Luis Barragán: The Phoenix Papers*, 129.

53. Ibid., 78.

54. Emilio Ambasz, *The Architecture of Luis Barragán*, 105.

CHAPTER TWO

1. The discussion here concerns the *masajid* built in America during a period of fifty years, from 1950 to 2000.

2. This is significant since, in Islam, the kernel of worship (*'ibadah*) is *salat*, performance of which is rigidly tied not to a particular place or space but rather to a prescribed time. See *Encyclopedia of Islam*, 2nd. ed. (hereafter *EI²*), s.v. "*masjid*," "*musallah*." In the United States, the term "*al-markaz al-Islami*" (Islamic center) has been adopted, since the American *masjid* serves in an expanded role that incorporates all of these functions as well as many other civic functions.

3. For example, early, modest structures were built or established by immigrant communities at Ross, North Dakota, in 1929 and at Cedar Rapids, Iowa, in the 1930s. See Yvonne Yazbeck Haddad, *A Century of Islam In America*. An indigenous African American Muslim community existed in Allegheny County, Pittsburgh, Pennsylvania, in the 1940s. See Jameela A. Hakim, *History of the First Muslim Mosque of Pittsburgh*. Undoubtedly, early African American communities predate the immigrant communities, but they have so far been inadequately researched. Allan Austin provides us with an excellent study of African Muslims in antebellum America in his seminal work, *African Muslims in Antebellum America*.

4. The anecdote was reported to me by Imam Khattab of the *masjid* (Islamic Center of Greater Toledo), who overheard the truckers' conversation. The mosque of Toledo, Ohio (completed in 1983), and that of Cleveland, Ohio (completed in 1995), both attempt to replicate a fifteenth-century Ottoman structure. The double minaret that both buildings employ had distinct political meaning in the Ottoman world from the fourteenth to seventeenth centuries; the patron of a double-minaret building was often a government minister (*wazir*) or a prince or princess. For concise discussions of Ottoman architecture, see Ulya Vogt-Göknil, *Living Architecture: Ottoman;* Aptullah Kuran, *Sinan;* D. Kuban, "Sinan."

5. On the question of image, see Johann Jakob Breitinger, *Critische Abhandlung von der Natur, den Absichten und dem Gebrauche der Gleichnisse* (Critical treatise on the nature, purpose, and use of imagery). Oleg Grabar describes image as seeing and showing; see his "Islam and Iconoclasm." Also see Erica Cruikshank Dodd and Shereen Khairallah, *The Image of the Word*.

6. For two contrasting analyses of form — one in religious and the other in secular terms — see Abraham Edel and Jean Francksen, "Form: A Philosophic Idea and Some of Its Problems"; and Jaan Holt, "Architecture and the Wall Facing Mecca."

7. For an analytical treatment of the homogenous nature of Muslim art and architecture, see Muhsin S. Mahdi, "Islamic Philosophy and the Fine Arts."

8. For an extensive discussion of this point, see Franco Ferrarotti, *Time, Memory and Society,* especially his chapter "Memory, Context and Tradition," 63–81. Ferrarotti suggests that "there is no possibility of memory without tradition." His argument was adumbrated by S. Alexander, who had dealt with the problem earlier. See S. Alexander, *Space, Time and Deity,* esp. 1:208–262.

9. The symbolic elements of church and synagogue architecture also render visual identity to the adherents of those faiths. The issue of Christian aesthetics and the contemporary church as a design problem also presents us with an interesting discussion. See Botond Bognar, "The Church and Its Spirit of Place"; Mark Alden Branch, "Inquiry: Religious Buildings"; Frank Burch Brown, *Religious Aesthetics: A Theological Study of Making and Meaning;* James Alfred Martin Jr., *Beauty and Holiness.*

10. For further discussion of the Muslim diaspora community, see Yvonne Yazbeck Haddad and Adair T. Lummis, *Islamic Values in the United States;* E. Allen Richardson, *Islamic Cultures in North America;* Kathleen M. Moore, *Al-Mughtaribun.*

11. Arabic sources tell of no inscriptions in the Prophet's *masjid* at Madinah during his lifetime or in the period of the four righteous caliphs. See Bisheh, "The Mosque of the Prophet." Many West African *masajid* follow the principle employed at Madinah owing to their similarity in construction. For an analysis of the West African mosque, see Prussin, *Hatumere;* Kahera, "The Architecture of the West African Mosque"; Fabrizio Ago, *Moschee in Adobe.*

12. For two opposing analyses of the expressive qualities of a contemporary *masjid* and the use of precedent, see architect Abdel Wahed el-Wakil's discussion of the problem in "Abdel Wahed Talks to *Al-Muhandis*" and the discussion by the Italian architect of the Rome *masjid,* Paulo Portugesi, in Carmen Andriani's "The Mosque and the Islamic Center in Rome."

13. These and other questions have been investigated in Yasir Sakr, "The Mosque between Modernity and Tradition: A Study of Recent Designs of Mosque Architecture in the Muslim World." See also Martin Frishman and Hasan Uddin Khan, *The Mosque: History, Architectural Development and Regional Diversity.*

14. *Sahih al-Bukhari,* vol. 1, book 7, no. 331.

15. For an excellent discussion of the cosmological order, see Titus Burckhardt, *The Art of Islam: Language and Meaning,* esp. 56–76; Issam El-Said, *Islamic Art and Architecture: The System of Geometric Design.*

16. For an extensive discussion of the question of perception, see Oleg Grabar's "Symbols and Signs in Islamic Architecture."

17. The Prophet's *masjid* originally faced Jerusalem, but a divine injunction in the second year of the migration to Madinah changed the direction to Makkah. See Q. 2:142–145, 149–150; see also *EI²,* s.v. "qiblah."

18. The formative principles of belief, order, space, materials, and symbols, described in the text, are unrelated to the Vitruvian principles of firmness, commodity, and delight (*firmitas, utilitas,* and *venustas*) spelled out by Vitruvius in his *Ten Books on Architecture.*

19. Conceived in 1949, the building was inaugurated by President Eisenhower in 1957. Chronologically, the Islamic center/*masjid* in Washington, D.C., is not the first

masjid or the oldest to be established in America. Earlier modest structures existed. It is, however, the first in a major American city. With the inauguration of the Washington *masjid,* the year 1957 signaled a major turning point in the development of *masjid* architecture in America. See Muhammad Abdul Rauf, *Al-Markaz al-Islami bi-Washington* (The Islamic Center of Washington).

20. The Mamluks were a military dynasty who ruled Egypt from the thirteenth to sixteenth centuries C.E. They were prolific builders. See *EI²*, s.v. "Mamluk."

21. The architect, Mario Rossi (also known as Muhammad or 'Abdur Rahman Rossi), an Italian Muslim, was at that time employed by the Ministry of *Awqaf* (religious endowments) in Cairo. He designed similar buildings in Alexandria and Cairo using the same design theme.

22. A tile-work pattern using decorative tiles from Turkey was secured to the walls of the prayer hall.

23. There is an ongoing debate among American Muslims as to the most accurate method for calculating the *qiblah* direction. See Al-Hajj Riad Nachef and Ashaykh Samir al-Kadi, *The Substantiation of the People of Truth That the Direction of al-Qibla in the United States and Canada Is to the Southeast.* The *qiblah* of the *masjid* in Washington, D.C., was determined by reference to the great circle, or the shortest distance, and the direction thus determined was northeast.

24. Q. 96:1–5, in the chapter *Surah al-'Alaq,* is, chronologically, the first passage revealed to the Prophet Muhammad. In translation, it reads as follows:

In the Name of Allah, Most Gracious, Most Merciful.
Read! [or: Recite!]
In the Name of Thy Lord and Cherisher
Who Created—
Created man out of
A mere clot
Of congealed blood:
Proclaim! And thy Lord
Is Most Bountiful—
He who taught
With the pen,
Taught man that
Which he knew not.

25. Anthony Vidler, "Type: Quatremere de Quincy," 148; italics mine.

26. The designer of the twenty-million-dollar *masjid* in New York (completed in 1990) explained that the client's design parameters for the building were dictated by two camps:

Camp A: the traditionalists, who demanded faithful adherence to a predetermined concept of the building dictated by historical models; and
Camp B: the nontraditionalists, who allowed absolute freedom in the design vocabulary but were rigidly conscious of the need to avoid violating any

religious principles (such as the blatant use of imagery) even in a minute detail.

See Stephen A. Kliment, "Manhattan Mosque."

27. The "six styles" (*al-Aqlam al-Sittah* or *Shish Qalam* = the six pens or calligraphic styles) are cursive scripts that were first raised to the status of major scripts when they were subjected to strict calligraphic rules by Ibn Muqlah (d. 940 C.E.). The names of these classical cursive scripts are Thuluth, Naskhi, Muhaqqaq, Rayhani, Tawqi, and Riqa. Other popular styles include the following: Nasq, Kufic, Eastern Kufic, Maghribi, Ta'liq, Nasta'liq, and Shikasteh. For a thorough discussion of all these styles, see Yasin Hamid Safadi, *Islamic Calligraphy*. See also Martin Lings, *The Qur'an*.

28. Kliment, "Manhattan Mosque," 97.

29. See Linda Safran, ed., *Places of Public Gathering in Islam*. The building was completed in 1983. Professor Gulzar Haider collaborated with Moktar Khalil, AIA, of Dana Associates, who served as the architect of record for the design of the project. Haider discusses the formative themes of Muslim aesthetics and the cosmological basis of belief in a very poignant essay entitled "Faith Is the Architect: Reflections on the Mosque."

30. Geometry is common to Muslim cosmology, and its many manifestations, such as *ramy, khatt, isbah,* and *ilmam,* can be seen in many extant examples of Muslim art and architecture. For a discussion of geometry and Muslim cosmology, see Nader Ardalan and Laila Bakhtiar, *The Sense of Unity;* and Keith Critchlow, *Islamic Patterns.*

31. Linda Safran, ed., *Places of Public Gathering in Islam,* 144.

32. Ibid.

33. Ibid., 123.

34. Umberto Eco, *Art and Beauty in the Middle Ages,* 58. Eco is citing Hugh of St. Victor in his commentary *In Hierarchiam Coelestem* (Celestial hierarchy) II (pl. 175, col. 949).

35. Traditionally, the *madrasah* is a type of boarding school where religious sciences are taught. See *EI²,* s.v. "*madrasah.*"

36. In the early 1950s, an indigenous Muslim organization, the Arab American Universal Arabic Association (AAUAA), had communities in Ohio, New Jersey, and Buffalo, New York. Remnants of one village community, called Izz el-Din Village, exist at Camden, New Jersey.

37. Hassan Fathy, "Mosque Architecture."

38. Ibid.

39. See Burckhardt, *The Art of Islam,* 190.

40. Renata Holod, ed., *Towards an Architecture in the Spirit of Islam,* 57.

41. For further discussion of this point, see Sibel Bozdogan, "Journey to the East: Ways of Looking at the Orient and the Question of Representation"; Ivan Zaknic on Le Corbusier's comments on the Blue Mosque of Istanbul in "*La Voyage d'Orient:* Translation of Le Corbusier's *Eastern Journey*"; and Christopher Alexander, "Battle:

The History of a Crucial Clash between World-System A and World-System B." I have discussed the question of the search for aesthetic truth while building a contemporary building in a traditional context. See my discussion in "ENPPI Headquarters Building, Cairo, Egypt."

42. One text that provides an interesting discourse is Manuel Toussaint's *Arte Mudejar en América*.

43. Again, this version comes from Juan Eduardo Campo, *The Other Sides of Paradise*, 56. I have included the second-to-last line as it appears in Bisheh's "The Mosque of the Prophet." The line does not appear in Campo.

CHAPTER THREE

1. Kevin Lynch, *Good City Form*, 229.

2. Peter Katz, *The New Urbanism: Towards an Architecture of Community*, xvii.

3. Lynch, *The Image of the City*, 4.

4. Ibid., 5.

5. New Jersey ranks fourth in terms of total population of Muslims in the U.S. The estimated Muslim population of the U.S. is eight million; New Jersey represents 4 percent of that figure, or two hundred thousand.

6. According to official statistics put out by the American Muslim Council, African American Muslims constitute the majority of the American Sunni Muslim community. This is true for Newark, as well as for many other urban communities throughout the United States.

7. This information was provided to me by the director of the Ashab al-Yameen mosque, Amin Nathari, March 2000.

8. The Mosque Scholarship Committee was started in the mid-nineties by Azizah Kahera, Khaledah Abdul-Muhaymin, and Salima Abdul-Ghafur.

9. For more on this discussion, see Robert Venturi et al., *Learning from Las Vegas*.

10. Ibid., 106.

11. Lynch, *The Image of the City*, 6.

12. Venturi et al., *Learning from Las Vegas*, 114.

13. Mircea Eliade, *Images and Symbols*, 34. Eliade comments, "The ethnologist has the right to declare himself satisfied with the results of his researches. But this is not the case at all with the historian of religions; for when once the findings of ethnology have been accepted and integrated, the latter has still further problems to raise: for instance why was it possible for such a myth or symbol to become diffused? What did it reveal?"

14. Epsilon Associates Inc., "Project Notification Form: The Islamic Institute of Boston," Section 1: Summary, 8.

15. See Lynch, *Good City Form*, 126.

16. See Lynch, *The Image of the City*, 66.

17. Epsilon Associates Inc., "Project Notification Form," Section 3: Urban Design, 10.

18. Ibid., Section 1: Summary, 4.

19. Ibid., Section 3: Urban Design, 9.

20. Ibid.

21. El-Wakil, "The Madrasah Mosque," 1–3.

22. Muslim Center of Miami Inc., *Muslim Center of Miami Project.*

23. Ibid.

24. Ibid.

25. El-Wakil, "Abdel Wahed Talks to *Al-Muhandis.*"

26. "Profile: Abdel Wahed el-Wakil."

27. Fathy, "Mosque Architecture."

28. El-Wakil, "Abdel Wahed Talks to *Al-Muhandis.*"

29. Herbert A. Simon, *The Sciences of the Artificial,* 25.

30. Ibid., 34.

31. Abdul Muta'al Muhammad al-Jabri, *Al-Muslima al-'Asriyyah inda al-Bahithat al-Badiyyah,* 16. The activist's proper name is Malak Hafni Nasif, but she adopted the nickname Bahithat al-Badiyya.

32. S. M. Darsh, *Islamic Essays,* 34.

33. Abu Amal Hadhrami, "Muslim Americans Need Own Outlook," 48.

34. Ibid.

35. Recently there has been a growing awareness of the real finiteness of public space in Muslim societies because of its social significance and its adverse underlying effect on sociostructural inequalities of habitat. Those who favor the total seclusion of women base their argument on the following verses: "O you wives of the Prophet! You are not like any other women. If you keep your duty [to Allah], then be not soft of speech, lest he in whose heart is a disease aspire [to you], but utter customary speech. And stay in your houses. . . . Be regular in prayer, and pay the poor-due, and obey Allah and his Messenger" (Q. 33:32–33).

36. *Sahih al-Bukhari,* vol. 5, no. 245.

37. Donald L. Miller, *The Lewis Mumford Reader,* 105.

38. Anonymous, interview by Neila Vora, Austin, Texas, March 2000, *The Functions of the American Mosque* (unpublished report, 2000), 5.

39. Abu al-'Abbas Ahmad b. Yahya al-Wansharisi, *Al-Mi'yar al-Mughrib wal-Jami' al-Mu'rib 'an Fatawi Ahl Ifriqiya wal-Andalous wal-Maghrib,* 1:229. For the history of Basta, known today as Baza, see *EI²,* s.v. "Basta." Basta was a small eleventh-century c.e. Muslim settlement (*rabad*) in southern Spain. It is located about 150 miles east of the city of Granada. Both groups pleaded their case to establish only one congregational mosque for the *rabad* instead of two; the dispute came before *muftis* for resolution.

40. It would appear that Basta had two congregational mosques in which the Friday prayer was performed. Group A expressed a clear preference to have the prayer reestablished at the older of the two mosques. They entered evidence about a river—which apparently separated the two mosques—and the fact that there was a flood, which was taken into consideration. Group B disagreed with A's contention and argued that the older mosque was inadequate and constricted, so it could no longer

accommodate the entire community. Group B also argued that the community had been performing the congregational prayer at the most recently built mosque for thirty years, with juristic approval. Furthermore, the recently built mosque was three times as large as the older mosque, making it better suited to accommodate more worshippers on Friday. For a full discussion of the debate, see al-Wansharisi, *Al-Mi'yar*, 1:229–234.

41. The first *mufti*, Abu Umar Ahmad ibn Muhammad ibn Isa al-Qattan, was a *mufti* in Cordoba who died in 420/1020. He is the most famous of the three *muftis*.

42. The second *mufti* was Al-Faqih Abu Abdallah Ibn Abd al-Rahman Al-Qarsuiti.

43. On this point, Abi al-Ghalib referred to the opinions of al-Qassar and al-Lakmi. He said that Mohammad Ibn Hassan al-Lakmi allowed two prayers without exception. This was not Malik's opinion, but two other prominent Maliki jurists, al-Qarafi and Ibn Abu Salam al Qayrawani, allowed choosing another opinion, even if it differed from the standard consensus of the *madhhab*. They argued that people had the right to choose the easiest opinion for themselves (*maslahah* = in the public interest) because all the *madhhab*s lead to Allah.

44. The third *mufti* was Abi Abdallah Ibn Mohammad Ibn Abi al-Ghalib.

45. For a similar discussion about Fas, see Kahera, "Reading the Topography of Fas: A Discourse on the Semiotics of a Madinah."

46. Al-Wansharisi, *Al-Mi'yar*, 1:166.

47. Darsh, *Islamic Essays*, 23.

48. Ibid., 24.

49. Barbara Freyer Stowasser, *Women in the Qur'an: Traditions and Interpretation*, 91.

50. Darsh, *Islamic Essays*, 32.

51. Anonymous, interview by Neila Vora, Austin, Texas, March 2000, *The Functions of the American Mosque* (unpublished report, 2000), 4.

52. Darsh, *Islamic Essays*, 19–21.

53. Anonymous, interview by Neila Vora, Austin, Texas, March 2000, *The Functions of the American Mosque* (unpublished report, 2000), 5.

54. Ibid., 6.

55. According to Stowasser, it is by this argument that modernists attempt to prove that the Qur'an did not legislate the duty of female seclusion in the home even for the Prophet's wives.

56. Stowasser, *Women in the Qur'an*, 78.

57. See Linda McDowell and Joanne P. Sharp, *Space, Gender, Knowledge: Feminist Readings;* Debra Coleman, Elizabeth Danze, and Carol Henderson, *Architecture and Feminism;* Shirley Ardener, *Women and Space.*

58. After serving in the United States Marine Corps for thirteen years, Abdulmalik decided to study architecture at the Cooper Union. In 1976, he obtained his B.Arch. During his years at Cooper Union, he came in contact with the ideas of Peter Eisenman, Michael Graves, Charles Gwathmey, John Hejduk, Richard Meier, and other prominent New York architects. His ideas of space and form were formally developed during the six years when he taught architecture at King Faisal Univer-

sity in Dammam, Saudi Arabia (1976–1982). He has also designed several types of public spaces, including an urban mosque for Harlem, where he was born, and a generic congregational mosque for New York City, which employ the principles of the spatial *sunnah*.

59. Information provided to me by Susan R. Scanlon of the architectural firm Venturi, Scott, Brown and Associates Inc., 4236 Main Street, Philadelphia, PA 19127-1696, March 2000.

60. Paul Waldo Schwartz, *Cubism*, 7.

61. Ibid., 12.

62. Peter Eisenman et al., *Five Architects*, 7.

63. Prussin, *Hatumere: Islamic Design in West Africa*, 149.

64. Denis Gril, "Love Letters to the Ka'ba," 41. Cf. Ibn 'Arabi, *Al-Futuhat al-Makkiya*, 5:1–12.

65. Gril, "Love Letters to the Ka'ba," 45.

66. Latif Abdulmalik, conversation with the author, Brooklyn, N.Y., 29 February 2000.

67. Ibid.

68. Latif Abdulmalik, *The Force of Space on Form via the Qur'an*.

69. Ibid.

70. Abdulmalik, conversation with the author.

CONCLUSION

1. Ismail al-Farouqi, *Tawhid: Its Implications for Thought and Life*, 240, 235–6.

2. See Doris Behrens-Abouseif, *Beauty in Arabic Culture*.

3. For example, see Michael Gomez, "Muslims in Early America."

4. Sylviane A. Diouf, *Servants of Allah*. The religious practice of the African American Muslim slave community has recently received much literary attention, although much more research awaits serious scholarship.

5. Gwendolyn Wright, "Places for Worship, Places for Community."

6. I asked one scholar of Islamic art and architecture to explain to me the reason for this neglect. He said that "there was not enough information available."

7. Mervyn Hiskett, *The Development of Islam in West Africa*, 13, 22.

8. Barbara Daly Metcalf, *Making Muslim Space in North America and Europe*, 131, 186, 204; Kathleen M. Moore, *Al-Mughtaribun*, esp. 117–184.

9. Gulzar Haider, "Brother in Islam, Please Draw Us a Mosque: Muslims in the West: A Personal Account," 162.

10. Ibid., 164.

11. Oleg Grabar, "From the Past into the Future: On Two Designs for State Mosques," 150.

12. Ibid.

13. Frank Burch Brown, *Religious Aesthetics: A Theological Study of Making and Meaning*, 21.

14. See Claude Levi-Strauss, *Structural Anthropology,* 301–302.
15. Le Corbusier, *Journey to the East,* 104, 110.
16. Rabia Van Hattum, "Ranchos Mosque: A Memoir," 1.
17. Ibid., 4.
18. Jaan Holt, "Architecture and the Wall Facing Mecca," 25.
19. Ibid.

GLOSSARY

ADHAN: The call to prayer.

AHKAM (pl. HUKUM): Laws, values, ordinances.

ALLAH: Arabic for God, the Creator of the universe; the sole deity whom Muslims must worship.

AQL: Intellect, rationality, reason.

BARAKAH: Divine grace.

BASMALAH: The statement at the beginning of each *surah* of the Qur'an (except *surah* 9), which reads, "In the Name of Allah the Merciful the Compassionate"; also used by Muslims as an invocation.

BATIN: The inner concept of being.

BID'A: Innovation.

DIN: A dogma or religious system; used in the Qur'an to refer to specific beliefs and practices.

DU'A: Informal supplication.

FATWA: An authoritative legal opinion contrived by a *mufti*.

FIQH (sing. FAQIH): Jurisprudence; the science of Islamic law, which falls under the purview of the jurists or *fuqahah*.

FITRAH: Natural tendency, innate character, temperament, or natural disposition; truth and order.

HADITH: A tradition, saying, narrative, or written report of actions attributed to the Prophet Muhammad; the source of material for the *sunnah*. Regarded as a source of Islamic law.

HAJJ: The pilgrimage to Makkah performed during the twelfth month of the Islamic lunar calendar; one of the five pillars of Islam.

HALAL: That which is beneficial or not forbidden by Islamic law.

HANAFI MADHHAB: A *sunni* canonical school of law, which draws its eponym from the founder of the school, Abu Hanifah (d. 147/767).

HANBALI MADHHAB: A *sunni* canonical school of law, which draws its eponym from the founder of the school, Ibn Hanbal (d. 241/855).

HARAM: Acts that are forbidden by Islamic law.

'IBADAH: Acts of worship or ritual.

IJMA: Consensus.

IJTIHAD: Literally, exertion; technically, the effort a jurist makes in order to deduce the law that is not self-evident from its sources.

IKTILAF: Juristic disagreement.

'ILM: Religious science, knowledge.

IMAM: A prayer leader who is designated to lead any of the formal prayers; in America, a director of a *masjid* or Islamic center.

ISLAM: Submission to divine will or purpose.

IWAN: Roofed or vaulted hall open at one end.

JA'FARI MADHHAB: The primary Shi'i canonical school of law.

JAMAL (capitalized AL-JAMAL):   Beauty; an attribute of or name for God.

JAMI: Literally, what brings together; congregational mosque where the Friday prayer is performed.

KA'BAH: The sacred black cube-shaped structure located in the mosque at Makkah. Abraham and Ismail rebuilt the Ka'bah after Adam as a symbol of monotheism.

KHATIB: The speaker who delivers the *khutbah* (exhortation) at the time of congregational worship on Fridays.

KHATT: Arabic calligraphy using one or more of the six major styles—Thuluth, Naskhi, Muhaqqaq, Rayhani, Tawqi, and Riqa—or other popular script styles.

MADHHAB (pl. MADHAHIB):   A juristic or theological school.

MADRASAH: A school for teaching religious as well as secular subjects.

MALIKI MADHHAB: A *sunni* canonical school of law, which draws its eponym from the founder of the school, Imam Malik (d. 179/795).

MAQAM: Station or place of standing.

MAQ'AD: The place of sitting on the *minbar*.

MARKAZ AL-ISLAMI: Islamic center; a building complex that consists of a mosque, classrooms, a book store, a cultural center, a religious library, and ancillary facilities. For example, the Islamic Cultural Center of New York and the Islamic Cultural Center of Washington, D.C.

MASHRABIYYAH: Patterned screen.

MASJID (pl. MASAJID):   Mosque; a place of congregational gathering, education, and religious activities.

MASLAHAH: Consideration of public interest.

MIHRAB: A prayer niche indicating the direction of Makkah.

MINARET: An elevated tower integrated into the architecture of a mosque from where the call to prayer was pronounced in earlier times. Today a public address system is used.

MINBAR (pronounced "mimbar"):   A rostrum, pulpit, or platform of three or more steps upon which the *khatib* stands to deliver the exhortation on Fridays.

MUFTI: A jurist qualified to make legal decisions in matters affecting the *ummah* (community of believers).

MUJTAHID: A *mufti* who is qualified to practice independent reasoning or *ijtihad*.

MUSALLAH: A designated extra-muros prayer space or area that is not a formal *masjid*. In America, the term is sometimes used to indicate the prayer area in an Islamic center.

MUSLIM: One who submits to the will of Allah; one who accepts, professes, and practices Islam.

ORIENTALIST: One who studies the Orient; specifically, one who studies the Islamic world.

QADI: A judge who makes decisions on the basis of the *shari'ah*.

QIBLAH: The direction of the Ka'bah and Makkah. Worshippers must face Makkah during the ritual performance of prayer; all mosques have a *mihrab* that indicates the direction of Makkah.

QIYAS: Juridical analogy; analogical reasoning.

AL-QUR'AN: The sacred text of Islam; literally translated as recitation or reading.

RAK'A: The cycles of postures of prayer (*salat*), i.e., standing, bowing, prostration, sitting.

RIWAQ: Hypostyle hall with regularly spaced columns and arches.

SAHN: Courtyard.

SALAT AL-JUM'AH: The Friday congregational prayer.

SHAFI'I MADHHAB: A *sunni* canonical school of law, which draws its eponym from the founder of the school, Imam Shafi'i (d. 204/819).

SHAHADA: The Declaration of Faith: "There is no God except Allah and Muhammad is the Prophet of Allah." One of the five pillars of Islam.

SHARI'AH: The religious law derived from four sources of law in *sunni* Islam: Qur'an, sunnah, qiyas, and ijma.

SHIRK: Polytheism; the opposite of monotheism.

storefront MASJID: A small mosque or *musallah* that can accommodate a small local or neighborhood gathering.

SUJUD: A derivative of the Arabic verb *sa-ja-da* = "to prostrate"; the noun *masjid*, often translated as "mosque," is derived from *sujud*.

SUNNAH: Practice, custom, personal mannerism, model, convention, law, habit, etc.

TAFSIR (also TA'WIL):   Exegesis, interpretation, or commentary of the Qur'an concerning matters of grammar; clarifying textual allegorical meaning, including the study of philology, lexicography, etc.

TAUHID: The Islamic principle of monotheism, which acknowledges Allah as the sole creator of the universe.

ULAMA (sing. 'ALIM):   Jurists; doctors of law and Qur'anic sciences, including specialists in theology, *hadith,* and other categories of scholarship.

UMMAH: Community of believers.

'URF: Custom, habit, and agreement.

WAHY: Divine guidance.

WUDU: Ablutions performed by a worshipper before prayer.

ZIYADAH: Extra-muros space.

ZULLAH: Shaded portico.

BIBLIOGRAPHY

Abdulmalik, Latif. *The Force of Space on Form via the Qur'an.* Unpublished manuscript, n.d.

Abdul Rauf, Muhammad. *Al-Markaz al-Islami bi-Washington* (The Islamic Center of Washington). Washington, D.C.: Colortone Press, 1978.

Ago, Fabrizio. *Moschee in Adobe.* Rome: Edizioni Kappa, 1982.

Alexander, Christopher. "Battle: The History of a Crucial Clash between World-System A and World-System B." *Japan Architect* 8508 (1985): 15–36.

Alexander, Christopher, Sara Ishikawa, and Murray Silverstein. *A Pattern Language: Towns, Buildings, Construction.* New York: Oxford University Press, 1977.

Alexander, S. *Space, Time and Deity.* 2 vols. New York: Dover Publications, 1966.

Ambasz, Emilio. *The Architecture of Luis Barragán.* New York: The Museum of Modern Art, 1976.

Andriani, Carmen. "The Mosque and the Islamic Center in Rome." *Al-Benna* 12, no. 70 (1413/1993): 70–75.

Ibn 'Arabi. *Al-Futuhat al-Makkiya* (Makkan revelations). Cairo: al-Hay'ah al-Misriyah al-'Ammah lil-Kitab, 1976.

Ardalan, Nader, and Laila Bakhtiar. *The Sense of Unity.* Chicago: University of Chicago Press, 1973.

Ardener, Shirley. *Women and Space.* New York: St. Martin's Press, 1981.

Austin, Allan. *African Muslims in Antebellum America.* New York: Garland Publishing, 1984.

Behrens-Abouseif, Doris. *Beauty in Arabic Culture.* Princeton: Markus Weiner Publishers, 1999.

Bernstein, Gerald. "In Pursuit of the Exotic: Islamic Forms in Nineteenth-Century American Architecture." Ph.D. diss., University of Pennsylvania, 1968.

Bisheh, Ghazi. "The Mosque of the Prophet at Madinah throughout the First Century A.H." Ph.D. diss., University of Michigan, 1979.

Bognar, Botond. "The Church and Its Spirit of Place." *Architecture and Urbanism* 1, no. 160 (1984): 95–108.

Boyer, M. Christine. *The City of Collective Memory.* Cambridge: MIT Press, 1996.

Bozdogan, Sibel. "Journey to the East: Ways of Looking at the Orient and the Question of Representation." Parts 1 and 2. *Journal of Architectural Education* 41 (1988): 38–45; 43 (1989): 63–64.

Branch, Mark Alden. "Inquiry: Religious Buildings." *Progressive Architecture* 71, no. 13 (1990): 78–85.

Bravmann, Rene. *Islam and Tribal Arts in West Africa.* London: Cambridge University Press, 1974.

Breitinger, Johann Jakob. *Critische Abhandlung von der Natur, den Absichten und dem Gebrauche der Gleichnisse* (Critical treatise on the nature, purpose, and use of imagery). Zurich: Orell, 1740.

Brown, Frank Burch. *Religious Aesthetics: A Theological Study of Making and Meaning.* Princeton: Princeton University Press, 1989.

Burchard, John, and Albert Bush-Brown. *The Architecture of America.* Boston: Little, Brown, 1966.

Burckhardt, Titus. *The Art of Islam: Language and Meaning.* London: World of Islam Festival Publishing Company, 1976.

Campo, Juan Eduardo. *The Other Sides of Paradise.* Columbia, S.C.: University of South Carolina Press, 1991.

Coleman, Debra, Elizabeth Danze, and Carol Henderson. *Architecture and Feminism.* New York: Yale Publications on Architecture, 1996.

Critchlow, Keith. *Islamic Patterns.* London: Thames and Hudson, 1976.

Crouch, Dora P., and June G. Johnson. *Traditions in Architecture.* Oxford: Oxford University Press, 2001.

Darsh, S. M. *Islamic Essays.* London: Islamic Cultural Center, 1979.

Diouf, Sylviane A. *Servants of Allah: African Muslims Enslaved in the Americas.* New York: NYU Press, 1998.

Diyab, Adib Nayif. "Intellect and Imagination in Ibn 'Arabi's Anthropological Epistemology." *Al-Shajarah: Journal of the International Institute of Islamic Thought and Civilization (ISTAC)* 4, no. 1 (1999): 53–75.

Dodd, Erica Cruikshank, and Shereen Khairallah. *The Image of the Word.* Beirut: American University of Beirut Press, 1981.

Drain, Thomas. *A Sense of Mission: Historic Churches of the Southwest.* San Francisco: Chronicle Books, 1994.

Early, James. *The Colonial Architecture of Mexico.* Albuquerque: University of New Mexico Press, 1994.

Eco, Umberto. *Art and Beauty in the Middle Ages.* New Haven: Yale University Press, 1986.

Edel, Abraham, and Jean Francksen. "Form: A Philosophic Idea and Some of Its Problems." *VIA* 5 (1982): 7–15.

Eisenman, Peter, Michael Graves, Charles Gwathmey, John Hejduk, and Richard Meier. *Five Architects.* New York: Oxford University Press, 1975.

Eliade, Mircea. *Images and Symbols.* Princeton: Princeton University Press, 1991.

Encyclopedia of Islam. New (2d) Edition. Leiden: E. J. Brill, 1960–.

Epsilon Associates Inc. "Project Notification Form: The Islamic Institute of Boston." Maynard, Mass.: Epsilon Associates, 23 July 1999.

al-Farouqi, Ismail. *Tawhid: Its Implications for Thought and Life.* Herndon, Va.: International Institute of Islamic Thought and Life, 1412/1982.

Fathy, Hassan. "Mosque Architecture." Undated manuscript. The Aga Khan Award for Architecture Archives, Geneva.

Ferrarotti, Franco. *Time, Memory and Society.* New York: Greenwood Press, 1990.

Fischmertz, Mildred. "Mosque as Monument." *Architectural Record* (June 1984): 142–149.

Frishman, Martin, and Hasan Uddin Khan. *The Mosque: History, Architectural Development and Regional Diversity.* New York: Thames and Hudson, 1994.

Gomez, Michael. "Muslims in Early America." *The Journal of Southern History* 60, no. 4 (1994): 671–710.

Grabar, Oleg. "From the Past into the Future: On Two Designs for State Mosques." *Architectural Record* (June 1984): 150–151.

———. "Islam and Iconoclasm." In *Iconoclasm,* ed. Anthony Bryer and Judith Herrin, 44–50. Birmingham: Center for Byzantine Studies, University of Birmingham, 1975.

———. "Symbols and Signs in Islamic Architecture." In *Architecture as Symbol and Self-Identity: Proceedings of Seminar Four, The Aga Khan Award for Architecture, Held in Fez, Morocco, 9–12 October 1979,* ed. Jonathan G. Katz, 1–11. Philadelphia: Smith-Edwards-Dunlap Co., 1980.

Green, Kathryn L. "Dyula and Sonongui in the Region of Kong." In *Rural and Urban Islam in West Africa,* ed. N. Levtzion and H. J. Fisher, 97–117. Boulder and London: Lynne Rienner Publishers, 1987.

Gril, Denis. "Love Letters to the Ka'ba: A Presentation of Ibn 'Arabi's *Taj al-Rasa'il.*" *Journal of the Muhyiddin Ibn 'Arabi Society* (Oxford, England) 17 (1995): 40–54.

Guillaume, A. *The Life of Muhammad: A Translation of Ishaq's* Sirat Rasul Allah. New York: Oxford University Press, 1998.

Haddad, Yvonne Yazbeck. *A Century of Islam In America.* Occasional Paper, no. 4. Washington, D.C.: The Middle East Institute, 1986.

Haddad, Yvonne Yazbeck, and Adair T. Lummis. *Islamic Values in the United States.* New York: Oxford University Press, 1987.

Hadhrami, Abu Amal. "Muslim Americans Need Own Outlook." *Islamic Horizons* 29, no. 1 (January/February 1420/2000): 48–53.

Haider, Gulzar. "Brother in Islam, Please Draw Us a Mosque: Muslims in the West: A Personal Account." In *Expressions of Islam in the Buildings of Islam: Proceedings of an International Seminar Sponsored by the Aga Khan Award for Architecture, Held in Jakarta and Yogyakarta, Indonesia, 15–19 October 1990,* ed. Hyat Salam, 155–166. N.p.: The Aga Khan Trust for Cultures, 1990.

———. "Faith Is the Architect: Reflections on the Mosque." *Architecture and Comportment* 3–4 (1995): 67–73.

———. "Islamic Architecture in Non-Islamic Environments." In *Places of Public*

Gathering in Islam: Proceedings of Seminar Five, The Aga Khan Award for Architecture, Held in Amman, Jordan, 4–7 May 1980, 123–125. Philadelphia: Smith-Edwards-Dunlap Co., 1980.

Hakim, Jameela A. *History of the First Muslim Mosque of Pittsburgh.* Pennsylvania: n.p., n.d.

Hiskett, Mervyn. *The Development of Islam in West Africa.* London: Longman, 1984.

Holod, Renata, ed. *Towards an Architecture in the Spirit of Islam: Proceedings of Seminar One, The Aga Khan Award for Architecture, Held in Aiglemont, Gouvieaux, France, April 1978.* Philadelphia: Smith-Edwards-Dunlap Co., 1978.

Holt, Jaan. "Architecture and the Wall Facing Mecca." *VIA* 5 (1982): 24–28.

Irving, T. B. *Mudejar Crafts in the Americas.* Cedar Rapids, Iowa: Mother Mosque Foundation, 1991.

al-Jabri, Abdul Muta'al Muhammad. *Al-Muslima al-'Asriyyah inda al-Bahithat al-Badiyyah.* al-Qahera, Egypt: Dar al-Bayan, 1976.

Jick, Leon A. *The Americanization of the Jewish Synagogue.* Waltham, Mass.: Brandeis University Press, 1976.

Kahera, Akel Ismail. "The Architecture of the West African Mosque: An Exegesis of the Hausa and Fulani Models." M.Arch. diss., Massachusetts Institute of Technology, 1987.

———. "Building, Dwelling and Reasoning: A Discourse on Maliki Law and the Ordering of Habitat in the Medieval Maghrib, 1400–1600." Ph.D. diss., Princeton University, 1997. Ann Arbor, Mich.: University Microfilms (AAT 9808389), 1997.

———. "ENPPI Headquarters Building, Cairo, Egypt." *MIMAR* 38 (March 1991): 68–75.

———. "Image, Text and Form: Complexities of Aesthetics in an American Masjid." *Studies in Contemporary Islam* 1, no. 2 (1999): 73–84.

———. "Reading the Topography of Fas: A Discourse on the Semiotics of a Madinah." *Al-Shajarah: Journal of the International Institute of Islamic Thought and Civilization* (Malaysia) 1 (1999): 75–92.

———. "Visual and Religious Arts." In *Encyclopaedia of American Immigration,* ed. James Ciment and Immanuel Ness, sec. 10: "Arts III." New York: M. E. Sharpe, 2001.

Kahera, Akel, and Gulshah Yildirim. "The Site Where the She-Camel Knelt Down: Exegesis, Gender and the Public Domain." In *Feminist Movements: Origins and Orientations,* ed. F. Sadiqi, F. El Kettani, F. Mouaid, L. Baghdadi, and S. Slaoui, 119–126. Fes, Morocco: Faculty of Letters, Université Sidi Muhammad ben Abdallah, 2000.

Katz, Peter. *The New Urbanism: Towards an Architecture of Community.* New York: McGraw-Hill, 1994.

Kennedy, Roger. *Mission: The History of the Missions of North America.* New York: Houghton Mifflin, 1993.

Khalidi, Omar. "Approaches to Mosque Design in North America." In *Muslims on the Americanization Path?,* ed. Yvonne Yazbeck Haddad and John Esposito, 399–424. Atlanta: Scholars Press, 1998.

Kliment, Stephen A. "Manhattan Mosque." *Architectural Record* 180, no. 8 (1992): 90–97.

Kuban, D. "Sinan." In *Macmillan Encyclopedia of Architects,* 62–72. New York: Macmillan, 1982.

Kubler, George. *Religious Architecture of Mexico in the Colonial Period and Since the American Occupation.* Albuquerque: University of New Mexico Press, 1990.

Kuran, Aptullah. *Sinan.* Washington, D.C.: Institute of Turkish Studies; Istanbul: ADA Press, 1987.

Leary, Alan. "The Development of Islamic Architecture in the Western Sudan." Master's diss., University of Birmingham, 1966.

Le Corbusier, (Charles-Edouard Jeauneret). *Journey to the East.* Ed. Ivan Zaknic. Trans. Ivan Zaknic in collaboration with Nicole Pertuiset. Cambridge: MIT Press, 1987.

Levi-Strauss, Claude. *Structural Anthropology.* Trans. Claire Jacobson and Brooke Grundfest Schoepf. New York: Basic Books, 1963.

Lings, Martin. *The Qur'an.* London: World of Islam Publishing Company, 1976.

Lynch, Kevin. *Good City Form.* Cambridge: MIT Press, 1984.

———. *The Image of the City.* Cambridge: MIT Press, 1979.

Mahdi, Muhsin S. "Islamic Philosophy and the Fine Arts." In *Architecture as Symbol and Self-Identity: Proceedings of Seminar Four, The Aga Khan Award for Architecture, Held in Fez, Morocco, 9-12 October 1979,* ed. Jonathan G. Katz, 43–50. Philadelphia: Smith-Edwards-Dunlap Co., 1980.

Martin, James Alfred, Jr. *Beauty and Holiness.* Princeton: Princeton University Press, 1990.

McCloud, Aminah Beverly. *African American Islam.* New York: Routledge, 1995.

McDowell, Linda, and Joanne P. Sharp. *Space, Gender, Knowledge: Feminist Readings.* New York: Arnold, 1997.

McIntosh, Roderick. "Square Huts in Round Concepts: Prediction of Settlement Features in West Africa." *Archaeology* 29, no. 2 (1979): 93–101.

McIntosh, Susan, and Roderick McIntosh. "The 1981 Field Season at Jenne-Jenno: Preliminary Results." *Nyame Akuma* 20 (June 1982): 28–32.

Metcalf, Barbara Daly. *Making Muslim Space in North America and Europe.* Berkeley and Los Angeles: University of California Press, 1996.

Miller, Donald L. *The Lewis Mumford Reader.* New York: Pantheon Books, 1986.

Moore, Kathleen M. *Al-Mughtaribun [Emigrants]: American Law and the Transformation of Muslim Life in the United States.* Albany: State University of New York Press, 1995.

Mugerauer, Robert. *Interpreting Environments: Tradition, Deconstruction, Hermeneutics.* Austin: University of Texas Press, 1995.

Muslim Center of Miami Inc. *Muslim Center of Miami Project.* N.d. Pamphlet.

Nachef, Al-Hajj Riad, and Ashaykh Samir al-Kadi. *The Substantiation of the People of Truth That the Direction of al-Qibla in the United States and Canada Is to the Southeast.* Philadelphia: Islamic Studies and Research Division, Association of Islamic Charitable Projects, 1414/1990.

Newcomb, Rex. *The Franciscan Mission Architecture of Alta California.* New York: Dover Publications, 1973.

Norberg-Schulz, Christian. *Existence Space and Architecture.* New York: Prager Publishers, 1971.

Numan, Fareed H. "The Muslim Population in the United States: A Brief Statement." (December 1992) *http://www.islam101.com/history/population2_usa.html* (date modified: unknown; date downloaded: 21 January 2001).

Pickthall, Muhammad Marmaduke. *Translation of the Holy Qur'an.* New York: Muslim World League, 1977.

"Profile: Abdel Wahed el-Wakil." *MIMAR* 1 (1981): 46–47.

Prussin, Labelle. *Hatumere: Islamic Design in West Africa.* Berkeley and Los Angeles: University of California Press, 1986.

Richardson, E. Allen. *Islamic Cultures in North America.* New York: Pilgrim Press, 1981.

Rykwert, Joseph. *On Adam's House in Paradise.* 2d ed. Cambridge: MIT Press, 1981.

Safadi, Yasin Hamid. *Islamic Calligraphy.* Boulder: Shambhala Publications, 1979.

Safran, Linda, ed. *Places of Public Gathering in Islam: Proceedings of Seminar Five, The Aga Khan Award for Architecture, Held in Amman, Jordan, 4–7 May 1980.* Philadelphia: Smith-Edwards-Dunlap Co., 1980.

Sahih al-Bukhari. Translated by Muhammad Muhsin Kahn. 9 vols. Saudi Arabia: Dar al-Fikr, n.d.

Sahih Muslim. Trans. Abdul Hamid Siddiqi. 4 vols. Lahore, Pakistan: S. H. Muhammad Ashraf, 1973.

El-Said, Issam. *Islamic Art and Architecture: The System of Geometric Design.* Ed. Tarek El-Bouri, Keith Critchlow, and Salma Samar Damluji. Reading, England: Garnet Publishing, 1993.

Sakr, Yasir. "The Mosque between Modernity and Tradition: A Study of Recent Designs of Mosque Architecture in the Muslim World." M.Arch. diss., Massachusetts Institute of Technology, 1987.

Sandford, Trent. *The Story of Mexican Architecture.* New York: W. W. Norton Co., 1947.

San Martin, Ignacio, ed. *Luis Barragán: The Phoenix Papers.* Tempe: Arizona State University Press, 1997.

al-Samhudi, Nur al-Din. *Wafa al-Wafa.* Cairo: n.p., 1955.

Schumacher, E. F. *Small Is Beautiful.* New York: Harper & Row, 1973.

Schwartz, Paul Waldo. *Cubism.* New York: Prager Publishers, 1971.

Sebag, Paul. *The Great Mosque of Kairouan.* New York: Macmillan Co., 1965.

Simon, Herbert A. *The Sciences of the Artificial.* Cambridge: MIT Press, 1969.

Smith, Jane. *Islam in America.* New York: Columbia University Press, 1999.

Stevens, P. F. *Aspects of Muslim Architecture in the Dyula Region of the Western Sudan.* Legon: University of Ghana, 1976.

Stowasser, Barbara Freyer. *Women in the Qur'an: Traditions and Interpretation.* New York: Oxford University Press, 1994.

Syeed, S. Mohammad. "Psychology of Dialect Differentiation: The Emergence of Muslim English in America." *Review of the Institute of Islamic Studies* (Faculty of Letters, Istanbul University) 1–2 (1978): 259–272.

Toussaint, Manuel. *Arte Mudejar en América*. México: Editorial Porrua, 1946.

Van Hattum, Rabia. "Ranchos Mosque: A Memoir." Unpublished essay. 26 Rajab 1416/19 December 1995.

Venturi, Robert. *Complexity and Contradiction in Architecture*. New York: Museum of Modern Art, 1966.

Venturi, Robert, Denise Scott Brown, and Steve Izenour. *Learning from Las Vegas*. Cambridge: MIT Press, 1972.

Vidler, Anthony. "The Idea of Type: The Transformation of the Academic Ideal, 1750–1830." *Oppositions* 8 (Spring 1977): 95–115.

———. "Type: Quatremere de Quincy." *Oppositions* 8 (Spring 1977): 147–150.

Vitruvius, Pollio. *Ten Books on Architecture*. Trans. Morris Hicky Morgan. New York: Dover Publications, 1960.

Vogt-Göknil, Ulya. *Living Architecture: Ottoman*. New York: Grosset and Dunlap, 1966.

el-Wakil, Abdel Wahed. "Abdel Wahed Talks to *Al-Muhandis*." *Al-Muhandis* 5, no. 2 (1412/1992): 78–79.

———. "The Madrasah Mosque." *Common Sense* no. 26 (Autumn 1998): 1–3.

al-Wansharisi, Abu al-'Abbas Ahmad b. Yahya. *Al-Mi'yar al-Mughrib wal-Jami' al-Mu'rib 'an Fatawi Ahl Ifriqiya wal-Andalous wal-Maghrib,* 12 vols. Rabat, Morocco: n.p., 1981–1983.

Wright, Gwendolyn. "Places for Worship, Places for Community." *New York Times,* 17 January 1999, pp. 37–38.

Zaknic, Ivan. "*La Voyage d'Orient:* Translation of Le Corbusier's *Eastern Journey.*" *Oppositions* 18 (1979): 87–99.

SUGGESTED READING

Bagby, Ihsan, Paul M. Perl, and Bryan T. Froehle, eds. *The Mosque in America: A National Portrait*. Washington, D.C.: Council on American-Islamic Relations, 2001.

Kahera, Akel, and Latif Abdulmalik. *Design and Planning Criteria for American Mosques*. Forthcoming (2003).

Murata, Sachiko. *The Tao of Islam: A Source Book of Gender Relationships in Islamic Thought*. Albany: State University of New York Press, 1992.

Pereira, Jose. *Islamic Sacred Architecture: A Stylistic History*. New Delhi: Books and Books, 1994.

Sardar, Ziauddin, ed. *The Touch of Midas: Science, Values and Environment in Islam and the West*. Manchester, England: Manchester University Press, 1984.

Serageldin, Ismail, and James Steel. *Architecture of the Contemporary Mosque*. London: Academy Editions, 1996.

INDEX

al-Aqmar mosque, 111, 112
Arabia, 46, 146
Arabic writing, 47. *See also* calligraphy
archeological studies, 53
architects, 8, 12, 15, 19, 20, 22, 37, 44, 46,
    57, 60, 62, 64, 67, 76, 83, 88, 99, 102,
    111, 115, 116, 117, 135, 137, 149, 150, 159;
    non-Muslim, 108
architectural form, 34, 38, 107, 113; bor-
    rowing of, 48; diversity of, 66
architectural theory, 4, 42, 44, 115, 150; on
    characteristics of a good city, 91, 98,
    106
architecture: history of American, 21, 54,
    57, 65; and Islamic law, 6, 22, 75, 93,
    121, 127; and landscape, 61, 93, 99, 113;
    and urbanism, 93
art history and historians, 18, 35, 37, 44,
    72, 88, 89, 133, 145–150 passim
asabiyyah, 98
Ashab al-Yameen mosque, 96, 97
Asia, 23, 48
atrio (courtyard), 56
Austin, Henry, 59
avant-garde, 8
Ayesha, 41, 121, 122

Baghdad State Mosque, 16, 17, 71, 135,
    162n.17
Bahithat al-Badiyyah, 118, 170n.31
Bait al-Maqdis (Jerusalem), 38, 40, 162n.9
Bamako mosque, 50
baobab tree, 50
barakah, 101
Baroque style, 56
Barragán, Luis, 60, 61
Basta, Spain, 125–126, 170n.39–44
batin, 77, 84
beauty, concepts of, 12, 13, 80, 117, 139,
    146, 152
being, Islamic concept of, 12, 84, 116, 117,
    143
bid'a, 19

Bilal, 101
Blue Mosque (Sultan Ahmed mosque),
    19, 20
B'nai Yeshurun temple (Cincinnati), 59
Boston mosque, 22, 92, 98, 99–107, 149
Boston Redevelopment Authority (BRA),
    99
Boyer, M. Christine, 106
Branford Place mosque, 92–97
Braque, Georges, 139, 140
Bravmann, Rene, 52
Buddhism, 101
building codes, 100, 101, 150. *See also*
    American building practices
building traditions, 5, 7, 34, 116, 146
Burckhardt, Titus, 84
Byzantine architecture, 46–48

Cage, John, 118
Cairo, 105, 107, 110
Californian style, 57
calligraphy, 47, 66, 69, 168n.27; Kufic, 47,
    69, 73; neo-Kufic, 69; Thuluth, 69, 73
Capilla Real, Cholula, 56
Cedar Rapids mosque, 147, 148
Central Asia, 146
China, 48
Christianity, 54, 101; aesthetics of, 54,
    166n.9; proselytism in, 54
Cleveland mosque, 26
Columbus, Christopher, 54, 57
congregational worship, 12, 19, 25, 35, 36,
    41, 44, 50, 63, 79, 91, 106, 114, 127, 135,
    153
container and contained, 112, 117, 138
Cordoba mosque, 30, 47, 48, 57, 91
craftsmanship, 114, 115; traditional, 69, 72,
    83, 116. *See also* sufi master craftsmen
Crystal Palace (New York), 59
cubism, 135–136, 139, 142; painters influ-
    enced by, 136, 140
cultural: conventions, 122, 150; displace-
    ment, 4, 5, 8, 57; hegemony, 5

Holt, Jaan, 14, 155–159
Hunt, Richard Morris, 59
hybrid aesthetics and traditions, 33, 44
hypostyle plan, 29, 42, 46–48, 56–57, 69;
    abandonment of, 31

'ibadah, primacy of, 67
Iberian peninsula, 54; Muslim architec-
    ture on, 57
Ibn 'Arabi, 2, 11, 13, 15, 137, 138, 141; theory
    of subject and object, 11, 15, 26, 150,
    152, 157
Ibn Hazm, 129, 131
Ibn Khaldun, 2, 22, 98
Ibn Rushd, 2
Ibn Siraj, 127, 128
Ibn Thabit, Hassan, 40, 88, 89
iconography, 13, 146, 163n.17
identity, 66, 72, 102, 148
ijma, 10, 14, 75, 123, 155, 158–159
ijtihad, 75, 76, 123
image, 65, 66, 69, 100, 110, 146, 165n.5
imagery, 27, 29
imam, 20, 110, 120, 123
Imam Baro, 51
Imam Shaw Kani, 131
immigrant Muslims, 32, 66, 72, 78, 80, 97,
    98, 120, 122, 124
Indian subcontinent, 66, 69
indigenous Muslims, 122
inscriptions. See epigraphy
Iran, 69
Isfahan mosque (Masjid-i Imam), 91, 111,
    112, 113
Islam, 3, 31, 32, 46, 48, 56, 75, 76, 80, 101,
    116, 127, 146; in antebellum period,
    18, 147; and Christianity, 54; in new
    contexts, 4, 51; in North America, 66,
    76, 93, 97, 121, 147, 158; spread of, 31,
    41, 54; and traditional cultures, 52
Islamic art and architecture, 1, 3, 14, 17,
    25, 48, 84, 145, 146, 148; history of, 53,
    54, 57, 63, 64, 74, 88, 112, 116; motifs
    in, 59, 87, 107, 133

Islamic Center of Cleveland. See Cleve-
    land mosque
Islamic Center of Greater Toledo. See
    Toledo mosque
Islamic Center of Plainfield, Indiana. See
    Plainfield mosque
Islamic cosmology, 12, 67, 73, 77, 101, 116
Islamic Cultural Center of New York,
    Manhattan. See Manhattan mosque
Islamic Cultural Center of Washington,
    D.C. See Washington, D.C. mosque
Islamic garden, 61
Islamic Institute of Boston (IIB). See
    Boston mosque
Islamic law, 4, 5, 6, 75, 79, 97, 105, 118,
    120, 128, 134; understanding of, 123
Islamic Society of Boston (ISB), 99, 102
Islamic Society of North America, 77
Islamic University of Madinah (Saudi
    Arabia), 97
Istanbul, 20, 153
iwan, 69

James P. Timility Junior High School, 104
Jeddah corniche mosques, 114
Jenne mosque, 48, 51, 53
Jerusalem. See Bait al-Maqdis
Jewish immigrants, 59
Jick, Leon A., 59
jum'ah prayers, 50, 79, 94, 120, 125–127.
    See also congregational worship
Jupiter, temple of, 48
al-Jurjani, Abd al-Qahir, 88, 89

Ka'bah, 38, 113, 117, 136–144 passim, 152,
    153; building of, 137
al-Kadi, Ashaykh Samir, 125
Kairouan mosque (Sidi 'Uqba ibn Nafi
    mosque), 31, 46–47
Kennedy, Roger, 54
khalwa (cell), 50
King Faisal University, 140
King Saud mosque (Jeddah), 114
Kong, 51

Muhammad, the Prophet, 6, 29, 35, 37, 38, 41, 52, 88, 118, 121, 130, 131, 155; companions of, 40, 89, 101, 109

musallah. See prayer space

Muslim: aesthetic values, 9, 14; art and architecture: *See* Islamic art and architecture; businesses, 94, 96; epistemology, 1, 2; feminists, 134; house (traditional), 84; jurists and theologians, 19, 120, 124, 130, 131; religious aesthetics, 1, 2, 11, 12, 16, 18, 19, 21, 22, 27, 35, 52, 54; societies (traditional), 15, 21; student communities, 104. *See also* Muslims; Muslim women; Muslim world

Muslim Center of Miami (MCM). *See* Miami mosque

Muslim Powwow, 82

Muslims, 82; early, 131; ethnically diverse, 94; non-Arabic-speaking, 66. *See also* American Muslim community

Muslim Spain. *See* Andalusia

Muslim women, 84, 97, 98, 123; access of, to mosque, 123, 128, 129, 130; privacy of, 130, 135. *See also* American Muslim women

Muslim world, 5, 18, 21, 64, 73, 107, 108, 123, 132, 151

Nachef, Al-Hajj Riad, 125

Native Americans, 56, 82

natural existence, 51

neo-Mamluk. *See* Mamluk style

neo-Platonic ideas, 139

neoteric composition, 12, 35, 93, 149

Newark City Hall, 94

Newark mosque. *See* Branford Place mosque

New Mexico landscape, 18, 84, 85, 87

New World, 54, 57, 62

New York mosque, 92

New York University, 97

nineteenth-century architecture, 54, 57, 59, 60, 101

non-Islamic environment, 78, 149

non-Muslims, 110

Norberg-Schulz, Christian, 139

North Africa, 48, 54, 146; mosques in, 56

North American environment, 1, 72, 78, 83, 89, 92, 93, 108, 120, 128, 149

Nubian building techniques, 18

Omar Ibn Sayyid, 148

Orient, 7, 14, 19, 58, 80, 84

ornamentation, 31, 33, 38, 46, 47, 56, 63, 87

orthodoxy, 42, 93, 123

Ottoman Kulliye, Edirna, 105

Ottoman mosques, 20, 26, 71, 153

Palladio, 86

patrons, 31, 32

pattern language, 14

Picasso, Pablo, 136, 140

Plainfield mosque, 77–80

Platonic expression, 136

poetry, Islamic, 40, 88, 138, 146

postmodern: architecture, 117, 138, 139; discourse, 133, 152; epistemologies, 14; theory, 35

prayer space, 15, 35, 63, 94, 106, 110, 125, 130; outdoor, 56, 97. *See also* congregational worship

precedents, 60, 67, 71, 87

pre-Islamic civilizations, 54

primordial man, 101

Prophet's mosque. *See* Madinah mosque

Prophet's wives, 122, 130

prostration (*sujud*), 38

Prussin, Labelle, 148

public gathering, right of, 15, 19, 121, 122, 127, 129, 155, 159

public image, 95–96, 106

public space, 91, 100, 139

Qadi el-Aqib, 137

Qala'un mosque/madrasah complex (Cairo), 105

Qarawiyyin mosque (Fas), 91

qiblah, 14, 34, 38, 69, 73, 102, 103, 111, 125, 136, 154; change in direction of, 40, 166n.17; direction of, 125, 167n.23

Qiblatain mosque (Madinah), 114

Qur'an, 1, 15, 22, 26, 33, 34, 36, 40, 41, 69, 77, 79, 84, 86, 106, 109, 114, 121, 123, 124, 130–133, 138, 140, 154; exegesis of, 125, 129, 131, 134, 141, 143

race relations, 93

Ramadan, 94

Ranchos mosque (Abiquiu, New Mexico), 45, 153–155

Ranlett, William, 59

rationalist thought, 16, 90

reconquista, 54, 56, 57

regional style, 5, 9, 35, 88, 92, 146; as adaptation, 29, 31, 40, 42, 87

religion, attitudes toward, 143

religious art, 136

religious symbols, 1, 89

Renaissance architects, 144

Romanesque style, 56

Ronchamp, 20

Rossi, Muhammad (Mario), 7, 68, 71, 72, 83

Roxbury Community College, 104, 105

Roxbury mosque. *See* Boston mosque

Ruskin, John, 117

Ryckwert, Joseph, 138

Safavids, 111

Samara mosque, 48

al-Samhudi, Nur al-Din, 38, 42, 122

Sankoré mosque (Mali), 137

San Luis Rey de Francia mission, 56

San Pedro y San Pablo mission, 56

Schmarson, August, 16

Schulz, Norber, 85

Schumacher, E. F., 86

Sebag, Paul, 46–47

secular and sacred, mix of, 79, 108

secularism, 14

Seku Watara, 51

semiotics, 2

Semper, Gottfried, 59

Shafi'i, Imam, 126

Shafi'i law, 120, 125

Shah Abbas mosque. *See* Isfahan mosque

Shaltout, Mahmoud, 118, 120

shari'ah. See Islamic law

Shaykh, 97

she-camel, 121, 129

Simon, Herbert A., 117

Simonson, Otto, 59

simulacrum, 28, 46–47

Skidmore, Owings, and Merrill (SOM), 7, 74–76, 150

Sloan, Samuel, 59

Smith, Jane, 3

South Asia, 146

space: conceptualizations of, 4, 16, 61, 139, 148; psychology of, 5; public and private, 106; sacred, 96, 107, 114, 115, 139, 156; use of, 4, 15

space and gender, 5, 15, 21, 22, 93, 118, 121, 122, 128, 131–134 passim, 155, 170n.35

space and time. *See* time and space

Spanish architectural tradition, 54, 57

Spanish conquistadors, 54, 82

Spanish Muslims, 57, 60

spatial ethos, 17, 19, 85

spatial ordering, 13, 25, 26, 29, 31, 33, 34, 42, 73, 92, 112, 121; of the city, 106

spatial *sunnah,* 6, 10, 11, 22, 27–36 passim, 41–46, 52, 53, 131, 155

spiritual values, 13, 76, 83, 113, 115, 159

Steffian Bradley Associates (SBA), 99, 102

Stevens, P. F., 50

St. John the Baptist, Church of, 48

Stowasser, Barbara F., 130, 131

subject and object, 29. *See also* Ibn 'Arabi

sub-Saharan African mosques, 31, 48

Sudanese mosque, 48

sufi master craftsmen, 84, 87, 116

Sulayman Palace, Jeddah, 114

Sulemaniye mosque/madrasah complex (Istanbul), 105

BAKER & TAYLOR